HE CALMED
TROUBLED WATERS

HE CALMED TROUBLED WATERS

by

SUZANNE WATERS-SUND

CONTENTS

PART III

PART IV

DEDICATIONS

I dedicate this book to my father, Frank LeRoy Waters, who passed away in 1977 at the young age of sixty-three, and to my wonderful mother, Catherine Heitl Waters, who left this world at the age of ninety-three. They were the most wonderful parents I could have ever had.

Much consideration goes to my siblings Patti, Jimmy, Kathy, Jeanne, Chip, Doug, Colleen, Donny, and Billy.

Sometimes, I could not have gone on without my two lovely children, Julie (Ryan) Twetan and John Ryan because I believe there was a time in my life when *they* brought *me* up.

Without my husband, Wally, and his Uncle Carl in my life, I do not know where I would be in my Christian walk. As minimiracles happened in my life, Wally would say; "Write it down for your book." So, Wally, here is my book.

FOREWORD

UTOBIOGRAPHIES are my favorite books. One of the best ever was Kathryn Hepburn's, simply titled *Kate*. I enjoyed reading her book so much because she wrote as though she were talking right to the reader. That is the way my book is. I will be talking right to you, the reader, as I relive my life.

Writing a book about my life has been on my mind for a long time. I started to write this at one of the happiest times in my life, on my forty-second birthday, which was November 12, 1981. I filed the beginning of my book away in my computer for twenty-nine years. Now, at age seventy, while my mind is still clear, I feel compelled to finish my story.

Just in case this book goes beyond my hometown area, I must tell you that all of the cities mentioned herein are located in the state of Wisconsin.

I have not shared my life with many. I think everyone has a story. Whether or not they share it with you is up to them. I have learned that you cannot judge a book by its cover, so I invite you to open the cover of this book and walk with me.

My parents are Catherine and Frank Waters.
From author's personal collection.

First, I will introduce you to my family. Next, you will see what life was like growing up in a family of ten children. Then, I will take you through the highlights of my school days. Finally, I invite you to walk in the shoes of Mrs. Ryan, Mrs. Meyer, and Mrs. Sund.

The last part of my book holds a brief summary of each of the sixty-six books of the Holy Bible. I created this for a five-year "Walk through the Bible" class that I presented to a group of dedicated people here in Waupaca.

Throughout this book I will relate to you how loving God, and learning to have a personal relationship with my Lord and Savior, helped me to heal during troubled times.

Acknowledgments

MY current life is with my husband, Bill Sund. I give him so much credit for putting up with me as I spend hours in concentration, writing my life story. He listens to chapter after chapter and has encouraged me to go on when I thought the task was too overwhelming for me.

Thank you, Shirley Richards, for being my friendly editor. You gave me lots of hope and encouragement. I will be forever grateful to you.

PART I

CHAPTER 1

ONE LITTLE, TWO LITTLE, TEN LITTLE WATERS

PATRICIA **Louise (Patti)** was born on September 28, 1938. Her middle name, Louise, is after our paternal grandfather, Louis D. Waters. As we grew up, Patti was always the older sister to each one of us. To this day, we all look up to our big sister, Patti. She is very smart and very poised. Patti is always well-groomed. She is a pillar in all of our lives. She married into a fine family at the age of eighteen.

Oh boy! It's another girl! It is I, **Suzanne Mary (Suzy)**, the one who came into the world like a tornado. From the very beginning, my mom said I was the lively one and probably the one who would cause trouble! Though I do not remember much about the early days, I do remember Mom telling me how happy I always was as a baby and toddler. Our neighbor, Mr. Oehlke, would comment on how I was always smiling and clapping my hands in my teeter babe on the front porch. I guess I must have been thinking ahead to my cheerleading days. He said, "She sure is a happy little kid." I must say, this entered my mind often years later when my life was in turmoil. I wondered what happened to that happy little kid.

꧁꧂

Less than a year after I was born, Mom and Dad brought our baby brother **James Brian (Jimmy)** into our family. His middle name is after Doctor O'Brien, who delivered him.

In our growing-up years, Jimmy and I constantly tangled. Recollections of Jimmy can never be forgotten because now, even the nieces and nephews have gotten wind of our antics, and every once in awhile, someone will say, "Tell us some Jimmy stories." With his permission, I will share some of those stories.

His favorite name for me was Omar. He said I looked like the picture on the side of the Omar Bakery Truck when I had my hair up in pin curls with a red bandana tied around my head. When I lost a heel on my slipper, he called me Omar Minus-A-Heel. Eventually, he shortened my name to Omar Minus. Oh boy! That made me mad; however, I think it was his way of getting even with me.

The new refrigerator incident stands out in my mind to this day. I had to open the main door in order to get to the freezer, which was located at the top. I had pulled the freezer door down. Jimmy was trying to pass by. Apparently, I was taking too much time. He gave the main door a shove and the freezer door went right through the main door. I do not know how long we were grounded for that incident. Of course, he blamed me, and I blamed him. That was how things went between Jimmy and me when we were youngsters.

Another time, I must have been taking too long in our one and only bathroom, which was upstairs. Jimmy was telling me to "move it," and of course I was not going to give in too quickly. Suddenly, he'd had enough and hauled off, and kicked the door. Since the door was hollow, his foot went right through. He tried his best to repair the door, but of course it did not escape Dad's eyes, and we both paid dearly for that. I cannot remember what our punishment was, but I do know that I would rather have handed Dad a new door.

This was not funny at the time; however, we have had many laughs over this incident. All I can remember is running as fast as I could down the street, while glancing back from time to time only to witness Jimmy chasing me with a kitchen stool waving over his head. All I could see was the lake in front of me, and it was getting closer and closer. Lucky for me, our neighbor, Mr. Chirstison, grabbed Jimmy, and I was able to get back home and out of harm's way.

Jim loves to tell this story. It was a Sunday; Jim had been painting the house all day. He was getting pretty tired of it, and wanted to go to the park dance that night. Dad said "no."

It was early evening, and Jimmy was watching television with the family. He had placed the ladder by his upstairs bedroom window because he had plans. Jimmy said he was going to bed. He went upstairs, quietly changed his clothes into dance attire, and proceeded to climb down the ladder and go to the park dance.

Now, Dad, feeling a little sorry for Jimmy because he had painted nearly all day, asked Mom to go upstairs and tell Jimmy he could go to the park dance. Mom went up, and lo and behold, no Jimmy. She proceeded to tell Dad that Jimmy had left, probably through the window and down the ladder.

When Jimmy came home later, the ladder was gone. Everything was locked up, including the airing porch door on the upper level. He and some friends had a fort down at the lake, and he went down there and slept on some cardboard. In the morning, as Jimmy came walking down the street, it was his luck to run into Dad. Dad just said, "Good morning," and drove off to work. I guess Dad felt Jimmy learned his lesson. Dad never said a word about it again.

One more Jimmy story: Dad was working 3:00 to 11:00 PM at the time, and he reminded Jimmy to cut the grass when Jimmy got home from school. Jimmy thought he had more important things to do; after all, he was a senior in high school. Dad got home at 11:30 P.M. and noticed that the grass was not cut. He went up, woke Jimmy, and said, "You forgot to cut the grass." Jimmy said, "I'll do it tomorrow." Dad said, "You'll do it now!" Jimmy got up, and at midnight, he was out cutting the grass! This was a push mower and not too sharp, so he had to go over it a few times! I recall how annoying that lawn mower noise was that night! It was a good thing we had understanding neighbors.

Unfortunately, Jim was diagnosed with pancreatic

cancer, and he had surgery in December 2009. We have grown closer than ever.

He knows I love rhubarb, and he has a whole field of it. When he brings me rhubarb, he calls it his "rhubarb run."

Jimmy knows the Lord. He has held Bible studies in his home for as long as I can remember. He is not afraid to die.

Frances died of causes unknown to me shortly after birth.

I have a faint memory of little **Margie,** the baby born next, as she lay in her tiny crib upstairs with vigil lights at each end, fighting for her life. She had spina bifida (an open spine). Mom and dad had her on her tummy with a shoebox over the opening on her spine. They knew she was going to die, but they wanted her at home with the family. There was nothing the doctors could do to save her.

Margie was so sweet, and I recall as young as I was, I would stand by her crib and look at her. She was so small and so helpless and she hardly moved at all. She never cried. She died after five and one-half months, quietly, and I distinctly remember the sadness that our little family felt at that time.

In 1944, **Kathryn Ann** came to join us. It was an exciting birth, because not only was she born very healthy, but my Mom's sister had a baby girl on the same day, and unbeknownst to my Mom and Dad, they named their baby Kathryn Ann also. Though they were cousins, we always called them "the twins." Out of all of the children in our family, our sister, Kathy, was the most compassionate. If one or the other of us were being punished or spanked for something, Kathy would sit on the stairs and cry. As of this writing, she is sixty-five years old, and she is still always the first one on site when one of us is sick or in trouble. Some things never change!

<hr/>

Jeanne Elizabeth joined us in 1945 and was the cutest baby. When Jeanne (six years my junior) was a youngster, she came up with the funniest sayings. We had a white picket fenced-in backyard, and that is where we kids spent many of our younger years.

Jeanne was around four when she came into the kitchen from being out in the sandbox. Mom said, "Jeannie, what do you have all over your face?" She innocently looked up at Mom and said, "Cheeks."

Jeannie also told Mom that she knew why God made dishrags with holes in them. Mom said "Why?" Little Jeannie replied, "So you can stick your finger through the holes and scratch off sticky food from the dishes."

<hr/>

Next came **Carl Louis—(Chip),** who was named after my Mom's father, Carl, and my Dad's father, Louis. He looked so much like our Dad that he acquired the nickname "Chip." That name is what most people know him by. Dad loved us kids and loved to hold Chip high in the air with one hand.

We were beginning to think the last of us had come. However, soon our Mom started to chew on Tums again. That was a sure sign that another baby was on the way. Patti and I were getting a little older, and we were given the privilege of unpacking the groceries when Mr. Ripple delivered them to our house. I remember both of us looking at each other and snickering when we saw the Tums. We knew Mom was going to have another baby before she told us.

Douglas Joseph (Dougie) was next in line. By now, Mom and Dad were asking us kids to come up with names. I remember suggesting that we name him Caboose, because he was at the end of the line.

If we asked him what his name was, he would say, "I'm Douglas Jofus." He was quite timid as a little tyke. I can still picture the following event: little Dougie must have been four years old. We had gone to Uncle Dave's cottage, and Dougie was sitting at the water's edge trying to touch the water with his feet. Next thing he knew, he was under the water, holding his breath, waiting for help. Soon, brother Jim came to the rescue, and according to Doug, Jim has been his hero ever since. Doug still does not like swimming.

Colleen Barbara (Colly) joined us next. I had a girl-friend named Barbara and asked Mom and Dad if we could name the new baby Barbara. Mom told us that she had a classmate by that name that lived on a farm, and Mom never liked the manure odor that followed Barbara. Poor gal.

They agreed to name her Colleen, with Barbara being her middle name. We always got quite a laugh out of Colly Dolly because she was almost two before we knew the color of her hair. She was bald for so long with the biggest, cutest, brightest blue eyes you ever saw. Yes, she was the beautiful, blue-eyed, blonde-haired person in the group. Pictures of our Dad as a youngster show him with blond hair, too.

⸻❦⸻

Donald Frank (Donny) was next, and he was actu-ally born with two front lower teeth. It turned out to be a detriment because he developed a nasty sore on the end of his little tongue, and the dentist had to extract those teeth after a few months. Donny was the one who asked mom for a honeymoon sandwich one day. She said, "What is that?" Donny said, "Lettuce alone." Donny was always quiet, but with all of us older siblings, I think he just could not get a word in.

⸻❦⸻

Our last baby, **William Patrick (Billy),** was born when I was a sophomore in high school. By this time, Patti was dating Bill, and I had a friend named Pat, so Mom and Dad let us name the baby William Patrick.

Billy was our pride and joy. We lived close to Sixth Street Park in Menasha, and one of us was always taking Billy to the park. He had curly blond hair, and he had the nickname "Curl" for a long time.

When Billy was in kindergarten, my daughter, Julie was just a year old. Billy asked Mom if he could take Julie to Show and Tell. The teacher approved of this, and when the classroom door opened, I was out in the hall to witness my five-year-old brother with open arms, welcoming my little one-year-old daughter. It was quite unusual for a five year-old to be an uncle, but Uncle Billy he was.

In his teen years, Billy started a couple of bands, and Dad allowed them to practice in our garage or in our basement. I lived in Milwaukee at that time, but I heard plenty of stories about Billy and his band practices.

CHAPTER 2

GROWING UP WITH THE WATERS' FAMILY

G ROWING up with the Waters' in a three-bedroom house in Menasha, Wisconsin, in the forties and fifties was accomplished with organization, lots of noise, and lots of love.

Jeanne's granddaughter, Rylee Alexis Craig
(from author's collection)

We always had a baby in the house, and we did not have disposable diapers. We had one bathroom through most of the diaper and potty-training years. We had hardwood floors and stairs. Dad said we should be careful not to put the wet diapers on the wood steps because the diapers would stain them. We managed to respect Dad's rules regarding this, but the stairs always had dark stains. Dad was constantly trying to buff and polish them.

Prepared, canned formula was unheard of at that time. I do not recall Mom nursing the babies, but I do recall her preparing formula and sterilizing bottles and nipples by the hundreds, and someone was always hollering, "Mom, the formula is boiling over!" Gads, how did she do it?

We did not have a dryer in those early days, so Mom would wash clothes in the wringer washer and hang them on the line. Soon, Dad tired of the perpetual clothes on the line and made a deal with my Mom's brother-in-law, Uncle Dave, who owned an electric appliance store. We soon had our first dryer. It ran constantly, and it was worn out within just a couple of years. From then on, our Uncle Dave saw to it that we had washers and dryers, probably at his cost.

I can picture Mom constantly folding clothes—diapers, towels, kids' underwear, boxer shorts, tee shirts, pajamas etc.—on our large kitchen table. Dad had made a top for our table the size of a ping-pong table. Our entire family had a place around our oversized table, and we would dine together every single day that I can remember living at home.

The little kids were quite gullible when Dad would point at the window, pretending there was a bird outside while we were all seated at the dinner table. All the little kids would look out the window, and Patti and I would see Dad slurp up the tomato bits and salty oil juice from his salad plate. Then he would wink at Patti and me. The little kids were still trying to find the bird. Mom would just snicker and say, "Oh well, it must have flown away." He did this almost every day. Wouldn't you think the little kids would have caught on? Funny.

This is precious. Mom made a braided rug by hand. It grew on her pregnant lap each evening. There were no television sets at that time, and we all would help Mom cut wool strips from old skirts, trousers, blazers, etc. Then, she would go to the sewing machine and fold and stitch the strips. After that, she would braid three pieces together. Stitch, braid, stitch, braid, and so on. Finally, she started to sew the rug. Night after night, Mom would sit on a straight back kitchen chair in the living room and put this huge rug together. It was an awesome sight when finished. It grew to cover our eighteen-by-twenty foot living room. We called it the "Technicolor Dream Rug." It was worn to a frazzle when Mom and Dad finally replaced it with boring wall-to-wall carpet in the late fifties.

Our living room was also our family room, gathering room, sitting room, playroom, den, meeting room, office, etc. It housed all twelve of us plus an eternal playpen: toys, toys, and more toys. When I was in my late teens, expecting a date, I would pick up all the toys and go upstairs to bathe. I told Dad, "Be sure the little kids don't mess up the living room because Joe will be here soon." He promised to be on the lookout. When I would go back downstairs, he would be sitting in his chair, snickering as all the little kids played with their toys. I did not appreciate any of this until much later in life.

My best friend from kindergarten through senior year, Nancy, had one sibling, a sister. Oh, how I envied Nancy. I would go over there; it was so peaceful, and the atmosphere was so grownup. She would invite me to their den. I longed for a den, somewhere to get lost in, where none of the little kids would find me. I loved spending time at Nancy's house. Nancy had a blazer in every color. I did not have any. When I saved up enough money to purchase one, they were out of style.

It was not until we were in our fifties, when Nancy's only sibling passed away, that I realized what I had with all of my brothers and sisters, nieces and nephews, in-laws, etc. I remember Mom saying to me that she probably would not be leaving much money to us kids because she was enjoying traveling in her retirement years. I said, "Mom, I don't care about the money; you and Dad are leaving us so much. We have nine brothers and sisters to share our lives with." It was unbelievable that when our Mom passed on, each of her ten children were gifted a substantial sum of money. Both Mom and Dad had done without things for all of those years, and they still ended up sharing whatever was left with their children.

While we were growing up, all of us kids had to share two large bedrooms. Each room had two walk-in closets and two double beds. The boys' room also had a crib. The newest baby slept in a tiny wooden bed in Mom and Dad's room.

Can you imagine twelve people sharing one bathroom?

There was twelve of everything: toothbrushes towels, wash cloths etc. By the time the oldest, Patti, was in her upper teens, Mom and Dad put an addition on to the house. They added a large master bedroom, a powder room, and a back porch.

In my early childhood days, we had great times listening to our favorite radio programs. I remember all of us sitting in a circle, listening to "People Are Funny" on Saturday nights. "The Bickersons" was fun to listen to, and so was "The Shadow," a suspense program. "Oh, Henry" and "Billie the Brownie" glued us to the radio at Christmas time. Later, we all basked in the fun of the "Jack Benny Show."

There were also times around the kitchen table when we all had to eat in silence as Mom and Dad listened to Gabriel Heater and the evening news. That was in the time of World War II, and Franklin D. Roosevelt had some serious news to tell our folks. We were a little too young to know what was actually happening out there.

Just before the war started, we used to have what they called blackouts. Sirens would signal when we had to turn out all of the lights in the house, and Mom and Dad covered our already blinded windows with sheets. We would light candles and just sit tight until the sirens stopped. This was a test to be sure if a real blackout was called for that we would know what to do.

I was afraid during those times. However, Mom and Dad just played their piano duets, and we all would fall asleep without worry. We loved falling asleep to the two of them playing "The Tennessee Waltz."

Occasionally, Dad would just sit and strum his

mandolin, and we kids would sing to "Turkey in the Straw" or "You are my Sunshine", while we waited for the lights to be turned back on.

The youngest of us all, Billy, was visiting his kindergarten friend next door who had just had a baby brother. He came home and said, "Hey Mom, how come we never have any babies at our house?" That was a good one and never to be forgotten by the older ones in our family.

This is funny, but at the time, I couldn't appreciate the humor. Dad had come home from work, tired and a little on edge. He took one look at our living room desk, which held all sorts of mail, bills, etc., and apparently, it bugged him that day. He took one swipe with his forearm, and all of the stuff landed on the floor. He looked at us kids and said, "Now, clean it up!"

Little Jeannie looked at him and without any fear said, "But you did it!" Oh my goodness, I am sure Dad got a chuckle out of that, but we all just grabbed Jeannie and told her to sit down and be still while we picked up all the papers.

One of my fondest memories of growing up on Frederick Street was when each evening, our entire family would leave the supper table and go into the living room, kneel down, and say the family rosary together.

We did this religiously each night. If we missed a night, we would say two rosaries the next night. Even well into my late teens and dating years, if a boy came to pick me up for a date and we were in the midst of saying the rosary, he would come in, kneel down, and finish the rosary with us.

Our Dad believed in the saying "The family that prays together, stays together."

When one of us got the flu, it went through the entire house. When one of us got the chicken pox, mumps, measles, or the like, usually all of us were down.

I recall days when we had to place a colored ribbon on the outside of our front door. The color indicated a particular disease and meant that our family was quarantined for a period.

One time when I was five years old, I was running an electric train for two of the little kids who were in bed with chicken pox. Suddenly, I fell over the tracks with convulsions. The little kids started screaming for Mom. Both Dad and Mom ran to my aid. Dad stuck an Eversharp Pencil in my mouth to prevent me from swallowing my tongue while Mom frantically phoned the doctor.

Occasionally, we had dresser drawer inspection by our Dad. Whoever had the neatest dresser drawer when Dad inspected got a prize. Think about it: we had ten kids and probably three dressers. Each one of us had a drawer, not a dresser. Funny!

Now, picture all of us sharing four closets. Our weekly inspection helped us keep our closets in order, too. How about this: ten kids, at least twenty shoes, of all different sizes, plus Mom's and Dad's.

We had so many furry mittens, big and small storm coats, hand-knit scarves, stadium boots with fur cuffs, etc. We had one nice-sized vestibule closet that housed all of these items. Luckily, we each had our own hook. It seemed that even though Mom and Dad tried so hard to keep order on the front, our house was always in chaos. One time, when a girlfriend walked me home from school and the house seemed unusually torn apart, I told her that our

Mom was housecleaning. It was not a lie; Mom was always housecleaning. She would just get finished cleaning one area, and the next area was calling.

Our Mom wore many hats. I was about ten years old when Mom got a part-time job at the local bakery. She used to bring home lots of big brown bags filled with day-old bakery. We loved digging in and especially loved the raspberry-filled sugar donuts.

Every Saturday morning, all ten of us were drawn as if by a magnet by the sound of the squeaky brakes on Grandpa Heitl's car. Each of us would drop whatever we were doing and dash madly to the door for the special bags of treats. There were Cracker Jacks, Oreos, Twinkies, Popsicles, Dixie Cups of ice cream, graham crackers, licorice, and gumdrops. These things were never on Mom's grocery list, but our jolly Grandpa always came through for us.

As youngsters, we loved to go to the public swimming pool at Second Street Park. Our Dad called it the pee pond. On hot summer days, we would beg to go to the pee pond, but Dad would simply say, "No, it's polio season, and don't ask again." Once in awhile, I would sneak over to the pee pond with Patsy Gosz, but it was always too crowded for us. I guess Dad was right; he was always right about everything, including the name of that pool. None of us ever got crippling polio, perhaps thanks to Dad's rule. He was right again.

The Waters' kids love watermelon.
From author's personal collection

We had a birthday at our house nearly every month. Mother's Day is in May, and so is our Mom's birthday. Father's Day is in June, and so is our Dad's birthday. Don was born in July, Kathy in August, Patti in September, Dougie in October, Suzy, Jimmy and Chip in November, and Jeannie was born in December. We celebrated our birthdays big. We had hats and noisemakers and lots of cake and ice cream, and sometimes we had watermelon. We did not need company. We *were* the company.

When we became teenagers, Patti and I were given housecleaning chores. One Saturday, she would have to clean the living room, and the next week, it was my turn. When it was my turn, I would always find a better way to place the furniture. Dad and Mom got a kick out of this. They always knew when I cleaned the house because their chairs were in a different place. I still love changing furniture and do it often. It gives a completely different look to a room.

Mom and Dad got a television set during my sophomore year of high school. The teens in our family loved American Bandstand. We would rush home from school to enjoy Dick Clark and his many guests on American Bandstand. We also enjoyed Annette and The Mickey Mouse Club.

While the younger kids enjoyed Sesame Street and other children's programs, Mom and Dad enjoyed watching Arthur Godfrey, Ed Sullivan, Lawrence Welk, Fibber Magee and Molly, and George Burns and Gracie Allen.

Dad and Mom had friends who did not have children, and those friends loved inviting us over to watch their television because they had a colored set (Their colored set consisted of a Lucite sheet over the television screen with graduated colors). The Flannigans were always so nice to us, serving popcorn and Kool-Aid and enjoying us kids as we enjoyed their hospitality.

Dad taught us how to cook. One week, Patti would go grocery shopping with Dad, and the next week, it was my turn. The one who did the shopping cooked Sunday dinner with Dad, and the other one cleaned up the kitchen. I got so good at cleaning the kitchen that I taught Kathy and Jeannie how to clean it until it was spotless. To this day, one of them will say to me, "And I want this kitchen spotless."

Our Dad was extremely generous. It seemed like we always had someone extra living with us. Our Dad's mother, father, and sometimes his brother (Uncle Bud and

Aunt Dorothy) would find their way to our address. Our house was a happy home. We had everything we needed. We were always well-groomed and had plenty of good food on our table.

Mom and Dad were always canning something. We had a fruit cellar in the basement, and it was full of home-made canned tomatoes, pickles, pickle relish, chili sauce, jams and jellies, and bread and butter pickles. You name it, they canned it. I got the canning bug early in life, and I still cannot get through a season without canning relishes, tomatoes, jams, jelly, pickles, and more.

We lived six houses from Little Lake Butte des Morts, and in our later years, Dad got a boat for the family. He taught us how to fish and water ski. We went out on rafts that we made ourselves and paddled our way around the lakeshores almost every day.

Our Frederick Street neighborhood rocked with kids of all ages, and there were always babies everywhere. Our street was referred to as Diaper Alley. It was a great place to grow up. We always had someone to play with. We played Hop Scotch and Kick the Can almost every night in nice weather. We also played Chase, I Draw A Circle On The Ice Man's Back, Jimmy Crack Corn, School on the Front Steps, Jump Rope, and Jacks, to name a few.

We loved to sit on the front porch and read comic books until we could not see. Trading comic books with our friends was part of the fun. Just the other day, I picked up an Archie Comic Book and sent it to my sister, Patti. Comic books are fond memories, never to be forgotten.

As teenagers, we loved to sit in the sun. We did not have sunscreen; in fact, to enhance our tans, we added iodine to baby oil. That gave us a nice reddish glow. We did not know we would face unhealthy skin conditions in our later years.

We did not have mosquito repellent either. If we got mosquito bites, we just made a paste with baking soda and a little water and smeared it on the bite to ease the swelling and itching.

I made several stuffed cats from the old family quilt.
From author's personal collection.

I noticed a multi-colored, pink print, hand-made quilt on a pile of goods that Mom was throwing out. That quilt brought back so many memories. I took it home, washed it very carefully, and proceeded to make a dozen stuffed cats out of it. At Christmastime that year, I gave a cat, made of the memorable quilt, to each one of my siblings, to Mom, and to my friend, Karen.

Besides his regular job at Banta Publishing Company, Dad opened up a hobby shop in Menasha called Hobbies Unlimited. We always had the latest gadgets; be it pogo sticks, skates, scooters, bikes, or hula hoops; you name it, and we had it. On the Fourth of July, we had cap guns, snakes, sparklers, and all kinds of other party favors. I do not recall many fireworks, but we were happy with our small popping sounds that went on from early morning until well after dark.

When we kids turned twelve years old, Dad let us have a few hours of work at the hobby shop. He wanted us to be trained in order to secure jobs on our own when we came of age. We especially loved working on Saturdays after the Brin Movie Theater let out. The store would fill with kids. Our Dad not only enjoyed his kids, but he enjoyed all of the others, too.

In our teen years, Dad formed a Menasha softball team. The kids had uniforms, an annual picture time, and all the trimmings. He also started a local hockey team for Menasha. Once a year, he would have the entire team over for a wiener roast. In our teen years, Patti and I loved to spy on the team outings. Yes, every kid in town knew and respected Frank Waters.

Most every Sunday afternoon, you would find our Dad over at the Menasha High School grounds, flying his favorite gas-run airplanes. He was always thinking of things to keep the local kids busy.

The local outdoor theater was a family favorite. On any given Saturday night in my early teen years, one could find the Waters' Family at the outdoor theater. We had a Model-A-Ford back then, and it was packed to the hilt with popcorn, Kool-Aid, blankets, lawn chairs, and kids. Many kids! On a hot summer night, we would take fold-up lawn chairs, sit outside of the car, watch the movie. As we got to dating age, we were not permitted to go to the outdoor theater on a date. I could never understand why. Hmmm.

CHAPTER 3

MORE CHILDHOOD MEMORIES

I love the good memories we had at our house on Frederick Street in Menasha. I do not think I ever fully appreciated Mom and Dad—how much they taught us and what they did for all of us—until now. Writing my story has brought great joy to my heart.

Dad loved to trout fish.
From author's personal collection

I remember Dad going on a fishing trip with his friends. He was supposedly going to be away all weekend. That Saturday night the doorbell rang. Mom went to answer, and there stood our Dad with tears in his eyes and a candy bar for each of us. He said he just could not stay away from his family any longer. Mom and Dad stood in the vestibule hugging while we kids munched on our candy bars.

Patti and I had to set the stage for the younger kids. We had to be home by midnight, no ifs, ands, or buts about it. Dad locked the door at midnight, and if we were not in the house, we were out of luck. Needless to say, we were in the house by midnight. Even when we were engaged to be married, we had to be home by midnight! We did not like it at all, but we abided by the house rules.

Prom nights were special, and because they were always chaperoned, we were allowed to stay out until after sunrise for our morning class picnic. It was all just plain, good fun. I was lucky enough to get invited to three proms throughout high school.

Bath-time at our house was a hoot. First, we only had the one bathtub for most of our growing up years. Saturday night was bath night when we were little. We would take baths two kids at a time, get out, add a little hot water, and another two would get in, We did this until everyone was clean. That worked out fine, and nobody ever complained. When we got into our teen years, we were shown how to use the shower and allowed that privacy whenever we wanted.

It was a Saturday night and I was waiting for my date to pick me up for my first prom when little Billy slipped in the bathtub and knocked his two front teeth out. Oh boy! My date arrived to mass confusion. Mom still managed to go to the grand march and take pictures in spite of the commotion on the home front, bless her heart.

School days started very early at the Waters home. Mom would wake Patti up around 5:30, and she would get in the bathroom. Then Patti would wake me and go back to sleep, and so on down the line.

If someone used the faucet in the kitchen sink while Dad was in the shower, his water would get too cold or too hot. Mom just said, "Don't anybody use the water in the kitchen while Dad is in the shower." We would inevitably forget, and Dad would bang on the wall upstairs until we got the hint.

We rarely had an entire night of quiet at our house. A baby might be crying for his or her feeding, someone might be cutting the grass at midnight, or somebody's bed-wetting alarm could be going off. That alarm would go off, and the kid who caused it would sleep right through the noise while everyone else in the house would wake up. That went on for a couple of months (or was it years?) until the bed-wetting stopped. Good thing that only happened to one of the ten, and I'm not telling whom!

I was twelve years old when my Dad's mother came to live with us. God rest her soul. Grandma had a friend named Walter. She had met him when he sold her an insurance policy. Patti and I shared one bed, and Grandma slept in the other. We used to fall asleep to a radio show that took call-in requests. Patti and I would secretly call in and request a love song to be played for Grandma and Walter. We all ended up snickering when the song was played. She laughed, too, and always denied her affection for Walter.

Patti and I would tease her by hiding her falsies, or we would move her glasses from her nightstand. She was always looking for something, and Patti and I got many laughs at her expense. Poor Grandma. Well, maybe it was just I that did the pranks, but I like to think that Patti was a part of my scheming.

We made up a song for Grandma, and some of the words were "Walter, take me to the altar." She would laugh and laugh and still be in denial. A short time later, Grandma said she was going on vacation. Dad and I were sitting in the living room one day when Mom handed Dad a post card. It showed a picture of Grandma and Walter, and it announced their wedding. They were old, probably in their seventies. I chuckled at the thought of her always denying Walter and his involvement in her life.

Mom made good school lunches. I can still picture her lining up all the bread slices. She would butter each piece and add peanut butter and jelly. The little brown lunch bags would contain the yummy sandwich, a piece of fruit, and an Oreo cookie or a Hostess Twinkie.

Our parents had a wonderful raspberry garden and concord grapevines that covered the back cyclone fence. We had grape jelly and raspberry jam aplenty. I can still see that cone-shaped, purple-stained, cloth bag tied up and hanging on one of the cupboard doors. We had so much grape jelly that at one time in my life; I could not even look at it. Now I just love it; it's one of my favorite foods. When I open a jar of grape jelly, I close my eyes, and a whiff takes me back to my childhood days.

The echoing sound of the 11:00 PM train whistle from across the lake soothed my soul. I would sometimes lay awake and wait for that sound. It was sort of like hearing loons on the water in the wee hours of the morning. I kept my windows open for fear of missing that favorite music to my ears.

Downtown was about fifteen or twenty minutes from our neighborhood. Early each morning, I would wake to the click, click, click of Mrs. Bunda's high-heeled shoes as she hurried to work. This went on for years. It was a pleasant alarm clock for me, that happy sound of a happy little neighbor woman.

Mr. Bunda used to let all of the neighborhood kids use his pier, and he allowed all of us to sled down his hill and onto the ice in winter.

There were many evenings when Dad and I walked down to the lake. We would cast for anything that would bite while we watched the sun set over the waters of Little Lake Butte des Morts. To this day, I love going down on our pier, here in Waupaca, and casting at dusk. Sometimes a big full, orange moon rising across the waters rewards me. I learned at an early age to appreciate the free things in life that nature provides. I learned that if we keep our eyes open from sunrise to sunset, we would always see something amazing. The beauty of nature can calm my soul for sure.

One summer, Little Lake Butte des Morts rose so high that it was halfway up that sledding hill by the Bundas' house. I would guess that hill to be around a fifty foot slope. That was very high and dangerous water, and none of the neighborhood kids were allowed to go near the lake until the waters receded.

CHAPTER 4

MY SCHOOL DAYS

OH boy! I wanted to go to school so bad. I was only fourteen months younger than Patti. I thought I should follow her the next year. I begged Mom, but since my birthday was in November, I was passed the cutoff date, and the school told Mom that I could enter kindergarten, but I would have to go for two years.

She enrolled me in 1944, and I loved both years. It's a good thing I went two years because in my second year, I met Nancy. We became best-friends-forever from that time on; sixty-five years later, we still communicate and see each other often.

One day I was walking home from kindergarten, and even though we were told not to open our report cards, I wanted to see what the teacher wrote. My teacher wrote, "Suzanne is a lovely child, however she is quite boisterous." I remember not being able to pronounce boisterous, but I was quite sure it meant that I liked boys. Some things never change!

My girlfriends would call on the phone for Suzy, and Dad would say, "Suzanne, telephone!" That made me so mad because Dad was the only one who called me Suzanne.

I never told him I didn't like it. When Dad died in 1977, I missed hearing my real name. I did not like the name Sue because of Johnny Cash's song, "A Boy Named Sue." Suzy was fine when I was younger, but Dad was right, again: Suzanne is my name.

There were so many times when my girlfriends would ask if I wanted to do this or that. Nothing bad, mind you. Dad would simply say no. As I grew older and started to be quite popular at school, I was embarrassed to have to say I could not go with them. However, little by little, Dad mellowed, and he gave us privileges relative to our ages.

I wanted to work at the bindery where my Dad worked because some of my friends bragged about how much money they made there, and I wanted to start saving for college. Dad would not allow his girls to be subjected to the negative language, as he called it, that flew around in the bindery. Dad was very protective of his girls. Thanks, Dad!

I don't remember our Mom ever raising her voice at any one of us. She was the gentlest person I ever met. Anyone who knew our Mom loved her. She was truly a Godly woman, and He watched over her and took care of our family's needs. She always taught us kids that God would provide. He did.

My Mom used to charge our groceries at Williams Grocery Store. It was right around the corner from our house, and when I was with Mom one day, I noticed that she had a large bag of groceries, and when she walked out the door, she just said, "Charge it." Hmm. That seemed somewhat simple, and there was no money involved.

A few days later, I took some neighborhood friends

into Williams'. We each got a cho-cho (a chocolate malt-flavored ice cream in a cup, on a stick.) Mr. Williams knew I was a Waters' girl, and I simply said, "Charge it." About a week later, Mom was opening the mail. All of a sudden, she said, "Okay, who charged some cho-chos at Williams?" Oh boy! I admitted it, and I told her I thought that all you had to do was say, "Charge it," and it was free.

One time, I took a piece of angel food candy from an open carton at Williams; it was my favorite. I loved the chocolaty aroma and the way my mouth watered when I bit into it. I put it in my pocket and ate it when I left the store. I knew it was stealing, and I have paid for that venture my entire life. To this day, I cannot stand to look at angel food candy. Though it used to be my favorite, stealing it left me convicted. It was another learning experience.

Dad worked with a man who had twin daughters just a couple of years older than Patti and me. The Fisher Twins had very nice clothes, and every once in awhile, we were given a huge box of their outgrown clothes. Patti and I were always so happy with the hand-me-downs from that family. I am sure our younger sisters were, too. To this day, I am always on the lookout for anyone who can use my clothes when I tire of them. I learned much about sharing from that experience.

Every year, just before school started, a big car would pull up in front of our house. It was a man who represented a clothing line. Our Mom would line up all of us kids and go through the clothing samples. She would proceed to order winter jackets, coats, dresses, tops, sweaters, trousers, slacks, and snowsuits, in all different colors and sizes.

Shortly before school started, we would get these huge boxes of clothing delivered to our home. We would all gather in the living room while Mom sorted out everything, and we would each receive our pile of school clothes.

About the same time of the year, Mom would walk all of us kids downtown to get new shoes. Tuchscherer's Shoe Store had an X-ray machine. We had our feet X-rayed in our new shoes to be sure of a proper fit. No matter what store we went into in Menasha, they were always happy to see the Waters' Family.

I can almost deem my teen years to be the best of my life. I sailed through school. My grades came so easily that I rarely had to study, which was a good thing because there was not a quiet spot in our home. My teenage years challenged me in that I felt compelled to get into every activity I could in grade school, high school, and beyond.

St. Mary's School went from first grade through senior year. Though I was elected class treasurer my freshman year, I never saw any money. I do not think we ever had a meeting.

Cheerleading started in sixth grade for me and continued through my freshman year. When I was a sophomore, there were tryouts again and I was elated to make the varsity cheerleading squad.

I felt very small in that first year of high school. The upper class students called us Greenhorns. I really did not understand what that meant until *I* was in the upper classes.

Sophomore year, I accepted a job as a soda jerk at a popular drugstore in town. I was quite upset when my boss-to-be heard that I made varsity cheerleader. He called me to say that he did not want another cheerleader on his staff due to conflicts in scheduling.

I was sitting on the couch in tears when Dad got home. He asked what was wrong. I told him. He said, "I'll take care of that." He called the drug store and convinced the owner that if he hired me, I would do a good job. He also said that he would see to it that I would be at work if I were scheduled. I was elated. My Dad went to bat for me. I held that job all through my high school years.

I went to St. Mary's Catholic School, and my coworkers were cheerleaders who attended Menasha High School. We worked out our schedules, and everything went well. The boss was happy.

My high school days were busy. We only had one car at our house, so I had to walk many places. Rushing to get to school, staying after school for play practice, getting cheerleading practice in and then running to the drugstore to put in my four hours was all part of a normal day for me. Many nights, someone called me to babysit, too.

One day while at work, a nice-looking young college guy came in with a girl. They sat at the counter and ordered sodas. He went to Whitewater University and had brought her home for the weekend. I noticed that he went back and talked to my boss before he left. I asked my boss who the guy was. Turns out, he was my boss's nephew, Jack. We eventually met each other and began dating.

I tried pleasing Dad more than ever. I figured if I were extra nice to him, he would be more lenient with me. I would wash the car, volunteer to go with him when he asked who wanted to go trout fishing or small game hunting. The boys were not interested, and I would always say I would go. We had good times, but I recall having to remind him on occasion that I had a date that evening, and I wanted to be back home by five. He kept his promises, and we were never late. I never regretted spending time with Dad, and after he died, I always treasured those memories. Having him one-on-one so often when there were nine other kids in our family always made me happy.

At that point in my life, I was a happy teenager, so involved in so many things and just sailing through life each day. I was on top of the world, so to speak.

Back in the fifties, I attended Park Dances every Thursday and Sunday night. The echoing sounds of "Cherry Pink and Apple Blossom White" could be heard within a mile of Smith Park in Neenah. It was always a thrill to be in that park at night under the stars, with scents of apple blossoms taking over my mind.

There was a live band, and we had the best music. Some of the popular songs were "Unchained Melody," "Sail Along Silvery Moon," "My Special Angel," "Oh Julie," "Sixteen Candles," "Chantilly Lace," "My Happiness," "Mr. Sandman," "Rock Around The Clock," "Blue Suede Shoes," "Mack The Knife," "Happy, Happy Birthday Baby," "Tequila," and "Over And Over." We had fun for sure.

A bunch of us always went to the dance, and during senior year, some kids would drive to the dance. Most of the time, we walked home after dark alone, and we were never afraid. I would stay at the dance as long as possible and then run home in order to meet my curfew. We were very safe in those days. No worries.

Gas was somewhere in the neighborhood of thirty-five cents per gallon, and a new car was probably around twelve hundred dollars. We used no drugs, had an occasional cigarette, and once in awhile, we shared a beer. We were good kids.

The beer-drinking age was eighteen at that time, and I was one of the oldest in my class. My friends would all chip in a quarter or so, and I would purchase a quart of beer. Actually, I only remember doing this one time. It was just with a few girls; we went to some park and all had a taste of the beer. Of course, we giggled, laughed, and thought we were getting tipsy. Someone always had Sen-Sen to clear our breath of the beer scent. I never really liked beer, but it was a fun time and just part of growing up.

I realized if I wanted to go to college, I would have to get a scholarship, a grant, or some kind of a loan. I could not possibly ask or expect my parents to pay for my schooling.

A friend of the family, Mrs. Tomarkin, told me about a scholarship that might be available to me. I gathered up all of the information I needed, got my I.Q. from the school principal, and filled out a mile-long application. I was granted a full year scholarship to Oshkosh State University. I was elated and felt very privileged to be able to attend college. At that time, with the experience I had with children, it looked like I would zero in on becoming a kindergarten–primary teacher.

Our senior class play was *The Queen's Gambit*. There were only two girls in the play: the countess and her niece. Tryouts came, and the girls were given both parts to study. I tried out for the lead part—the countess. After a week or so, I earned first chance for that part. The director made it clear that if for any reason I did not work out, they had picked Mary Louise to back me up. I really wanted the lead. I studied and prepared for it with all of my heart.

Because I had a ducktail, my Mom and Grandma Heitl designed a headpiece with black lace over a tiara to make me look the part of the countess. They also made a couple of beautiful long full dresses for me to wear in the play. I practiced almost every day after school and on Saturdays. The play was performed four different days with the last performance being on a Saturday night. I spotted Mom and Dad in the crowd and decided this was going to be my best performance ever. I "broke a leg."

After the play, Mom and Dad presented me with a dozen red roses and had a cast party at the house. I felt bad for Mom and Dad because one by one, the kids started to leave our house and head for the local teen bar. Dad just looked at me and said, "Oh, go ahead, just behave yourself." That was a first. He must have been impressed with the countess.

Having the lead in the play was truly a highlight of my high school days, and I was honored. I jostled between cheerleading, chorus, my part-time job at the soda fountain, the class play lead and babysitting. It worked out!

From time to time, my friends and I would take off for Waupaca for an event at the Indian Crossing Casino. It was a wonderful place for our age group to gather. Some of the top-notch bands played there, and we had fun attending those events.

Mom and Dad went somewhere for the day with another couple and all of the kids except Billy, who was the baby. Billy was born when I was a sophomore. They left me in charge of taking care of Billy that day.

One of my girlfriends called and asked if I could get the car and drive a few of the girls to Waupaca to look for a cottage we could rent for a week following graduation. I said, "Well, the car is here, and if you want to hold my baby brother, I will drive." I was glad I did not have to ask my parents' permission. Soon, four of us girls got in the car and headed for Waupaca. Billy would not settle down. It was nerve-racking to hear him cry, screaming all the way to and from our destination that day. It was like he was telling me I should not be doing this.

All of my friends chipped in for gas, and I was sure to have the gauge right where it was when we left. Though we were home before the rest of the family, I did not have to tell them that I took the car. Dad could tell from the odometer when he took the car to work the next day. We never got away with anything.

Dad, Me, and Mom (June 1958).
From author's personal collection

It came time for graduation from high school. It was a happy time, and I recall an event that was and always will be very special to me. Dad said, "Catherine, I'm taking Suzanne shopping for an outfit for graduation." Wow! I was so excited. We went to Jandry's in Neenah, and I picked out a white knit chemise dress and a red knit coat. It was the best. Boy, do I ever wish I had hung on to that. However, like all of our clothes, we passed them down the line to younger siblings.

Our class had the time of our lives on graduation day in June 1958. We had parties all day with relatives and friends and commencement services in the evening. The amount of money I received in my graduation cards surprised me. My biggest surprise was a twenty dollar bill from my boss. That was a lot of money in 1958.

After the evening service, my girlfriends and I went home to collect our packed suitcases. Away we went to Waupaca and the cottage we had rented at Camp Cleghorn on the Chain of Lakes.

After spending an entire week away with my friends, sans the little kids, I was anxiously awaiting my upcoming year at college.

I worked a lot that summer, earning seventy-five cents an hour at the drugstore. Every penny went into my college fund. Mom and Dad gave each of us kids one hundred dollars when we graduated from high school. I put mine toward college, but most of the others used theirs toward their senior class trip to Washington DC.

Jack and I started dating during my senior year. He was head lifeguard at the Menasha Swimming Pool. My girlfriends and I spent many days at that pool. The sailor dive was a favorite of mine. You place the right foot a little ahead of the left and extend both arms out straight. One time, while showing off my sailor dive from the high diving board, I dislocated my hip. I was rushed to the hospital by ambulance. I later realized that the sailor dive was designed for someone to get into the water quick and stay near the surface to help someone in need. It was not designed to be used from the high dive. Having my hip replaced in my mid-sixties sparked this memory.

Lucky for me, Jack was smart enough to tell me to date while I was in college, and we would see each other from time to time when we both were home on weekends, school breaks, and summer.

Boy! Not developing good study habits in grade and high school hurt me when I was in college. I was very lost when it came to studying, paying attention, and organizing my time. As a result, my grades suffered. Midway through the year, I knew I would not be returning the following year due to a lack of funds, so I decided to just have fun.

Also, to add to the lack of enthusiasm in college, I did not make the cheerleading squad. Cheerleading meant so much to me in high school, and not making the college squad crushed me.

Dorm life suited me fine. I had an adult life in the dorm. I had my own checkbook, and I was on my own. We had good, clean fun. We'd sneak each other into and out of the first floor dorm windows from time to time and stay at one of our classmates homes that lived in town, but we never got into trouble.

One time, the college allowed a man to distribute

cartons of cigarettes to anyone who wanted them in the dorm. They were free. Of course, that was before the Surgeon General's report that cigarettes were a hazard to our health. Dad forbade smoking in our home, but in the dorm, I could smoke whenever I wanted. Lucky for me, I never got hooked on them.

I loved being with the girls and being away from all of my younger brothers and sisters for a change. Though I missed the family from time to time, I got over it.

Occasionally, Patti and Bill would visit me at the dorm. Before they left me, they always slipped me some money. I'll never forget their generosity, not only to me but to our entire family.

Finals came and we all glued ourselves to our desk chairs in the dorm or the library for an entire week, cramming for exams. At the end of our tests, some of us decided to walk down to the Magnet Bar. It was a fun place for college kids where we could have a mug of beer and play the bowling game. Another gal and myself decided to borrow that little black bowling ball (which we took back later), and I recall bouncing that thing on the sidewalk all the way back to the dorm. We were just being silly and having some laughs.

Our fun came to an abrupt end. When we got back to our dorm (Emily Webster Hall-OSC was new in 1958), I stupidly placed my hand on the fire alarm, another gal pulled my hand down, and off went the alarm. Our dorm was three stories, and as expected, all of the students emptied into the cool night. This was around 10:00 PM, so most of the gals were in their pajamas. I filed out with the group, and already I was heartsick.

Everyone in our group made me promise I would not tell. Well after the fire trucks arrived and it was deemed safe to go back into our dorm, I started to cry and wanted to turn myself in. My roommate handed me my rosary and told me to go to sleep and just forget it. No matter how hard I tried, sleep did not come. It's called a guilty conscience.

The next day, we all went to classes, and the day started out quite normally. When we got back to our dorm after classes, there was a note posted on the lobby bulletin board. It said, "There will be a meeting at seven tonight in the student union. Everyone MUST attend. The fire chief will be here to speak to the residents of Emily Webster Hall."

Oh my! Now I was really nervous. My friends kept telling me it would be okay. The first words out of the chief's mouth were, "There's a culprit in the crowd!" Again, I wanted to jump up and confess, but I stayed put and just listened to him talk. In essence, he told us how serious and costly this prank was. My heart squeezed, and my stomach churned.

By the next day, after my morning classes, I was back in the dorm, and nobody could hold me back. I went directly to Mrs. Henderson, our house mother, and confessed to setting off the fire alarm. I told her I would not reveal the name of the person who was in on this with me. I never did. I was grounded for two weeks.

I also had to face the Dean of Men. I will never forget that meeting. I was crying, and he was reminding me that I was there on a scholarship, and this was not good! I kept saying over and over, "Please don't tell my Dad." That was my biggest fear at that point. I promised to take my punishment, write a letter of apology to the fire department, expose my name, and anything else that was required of me to repent for my serious prank. He accepted my offer to compensate. He forgave me and turned me over to Mrs. Henderson. Of course, I was grounded and missed several basketball games and other functions. I remember being quite humble during this time. I was pleased that they were not going to report the incident to my Dad.

One night, toward the end of my grounding, Mrs. Henderson saw that I was sitting in the lobby watching my friends build a snowman outside, and she said, "Suzy, go ahead; join your friends and have fun in the snow." She was a real sweetie and had compassion for me because she knew there was another gal involved who never came forward.

When the dust settled, Mrs. Henderson came into my room one morning and said "Suzy, close your eyes, and open up your hand." She placed the two pieces of the glass bar into my hand that had broken when the fire alarm was set off. She gave me a big hug and said, "These are for your scrapbook."

I learned great lessons through this episode. I learned to always think before acting, and, above all, to always confess if an error is made. No matter what the consequences, or what wrongdoing occurred, I had a conscious, and my heart and mind would not have peace until I confessed.

I always felt good about not turning in the other gal. I have often wondered if this incident ever came back to haunt her!

My college days were fun. However, in the back of my mind, I knew I would not be able to return the next year. No student loans were available to us, and there was no way I could expect Mom and Dad to pay my way through college. Midway through the year, I realized I did not want to be a teacher. I decided it would be best to return home. I made the best of my college days and didn't pay as much attention to the books as I should have. Now, at age seventy, I can't get enough of history and geography and all those other academic studies.

CHAPTER 5

FREDERICK STREET, MENASHA—JUNE, 1959

MOVING back home with eight younger brothers and sisters challenged me. I envied Patti's being married. Occasionally, she let me stay overnight at their house. I loved spending time with Patti and Bill.

Meanwhile, back home, Mom and Dad gave me a bedroom to myself. I tucked away a lot, listening to records, reading, or writing letters to Jack. Yes, we were hitting it off quite well, and every time he came home, he would call me for a date. When he invited me to Whitewater for The Rose Dance, I was thrilled. He was the king of the dance, and that girl he had brought in to the drug store was the queen. I took the Greyhound bus all the way from Menasha to Whitewater, which took nearly all day. Jack met me, and I stayed with one of his married friends for the weekend.

It was a very hot weekend, and after the Rose Dance, a lot of people gathered on blankets in the park, and we listened to music and enjoyed the cool night air until sunrise. Because he had recently broken up with that girl,

I felt very privileged to be with him, and I felt he was falling for me, too.

When Jack graduated from college, I attended the ceremony with his parents. He moved back to Menasha for the summer, and by fall, he had accepted a job in Milwaukee. He came home almost every weekend, and we got engaged on December 25, 1959.

Jack fit right into my family. Everyone loved him, including me. I was especially grateful that he loved me enough to ask me to marry him. Our courting days were fun-filled, and we enjoyed so many of the same things. I loved being with his family, and he loved all of my siblings and the interaction that came with a large family.

Though I was not too sure about moving to Milwaukee, I was glad to know that I would be starting a new life with Jack. It didn't really matter where we lived; I was happy, happy, happy.

I admired Jack's intelligence, and I knew he would be a good husband. I wasn't even thinking of having children. I was leaving a household full of kids, and I was ready for some peace and quiet. As I said, we were not allowed to even think about moving out on our own. This was going to be great!

CHAPTER 6

SUZANNE RYAN (SEPTEMBER 1960) —MILWAUKEE

JACK had already found an apartment for us in Milwaukee, not too far from his work. We only had one car, but he could walk to work most days, and though I didn't know anyone, I had the car if I wanted to venture out.

I loved being on my own with a husband in a big city, cooking meals and getting organized. Dad taught us that the first thing you do after you get married is build up a credit rating. We went to a furniture store in Milwaukee and bought our new furniture on credit.

We had a really cute apartment for seventy-five dollars a month, including heat, electricity, and water, and we had everything we needed. It didn't take long for me to become acquainted with people in our apartment building, which was on Humboldt Avenue. The river separating Milwaukee from Shorewood sat just across the street.

When an upper, front apartment became available for the same rent, we were glad to make the move. We could see the Pig 'N Whistle from our upper apartment window. The "Pig," as it was called, was a very popular place for good food and meeting friends.

We only had one bedroom and one bathroom. The dining room and living room were of equal size and very adequate. We had a tiny kitchen with a large pass-through opening into the dining room. We had a Murphy bed at one end of the dining room, and we used that for out of town guests.

We were happy in our front, upper apartment and ready to show it off. One day, I sat on our front window seat, which faced Humboldt Avenue. I noticed a familiar car pull up. After a minute or so, a man and lady got out. Upon second glance, I recognized my mom and dad. It was a wonderful surprise and made a fond memory: my Mom and Dad, with all those kids back home, took a trip to Milwaukee to see me.

We had a wonderful visit, and they stayed overnight. The following day, we took them around Milwaukee. Dad didn't like the big city, but he enjoyed seeing where we lived. Soon, they were on the road again. That was the only time Mom and Dad came to Milwaukee until we moved into our new house in 1965.

Oh yes, we were as snug as bugs in our Milwaukee apartment. However, it didn't take long for me to start combing the help wanted ads for a secretarial job.

I stepped out one day, on my own, without telling my husband. I was going to interview for a job at the New York Life Insurance (NYLI) company in downtown Milwaukee. I felt so grown up and ready to take on a big job in a big city. Well, my dreams were dashed quickly.

First of all, I could not find the NYLI building. Then, when I located the building, I couldn't find a place to park. I was quite turned around by the time I found a parking space, but I parked the car, locked it, and left. Now what? I had to try to find that building again. By the time I located the building, I was late for my interview. I finally found the office—on the top floor—after getting lost while looking for the elevators.

As I humbly apologized to the woman who would conduct my interview, she reminded me it was not a very good start, being late for an interview, I told her that I had made a mistake. She immediately took compassion on me and listened to this twenty-year-old young adult who had been misplaced from a small town to a big city. She sat with me while I dried my tears and got my composure, after which I quietly went out the door that I had come in.

When I got out of the building, I could not find my car. I was sure I had parked on this street. I looked and looked, but there were no cars in sight. Well, you guessed it! I had parked in a tow-away zone and had to jump through some hoops before I got my car back. I had no idea they had tow-away zones in Milwaukee. The policeman and the tow company personnel were very kind. I must have looked a mess, crying and carrying on about how my new husband didn't even know what I was up to. They encouraged me to calm down, go back home, and call my husband.

I got back into my car and realized it was after 4:00 PM, and I was in rush hour traffic. There were no freeways in Milwaukee in 1960. It took me well over an hour to find my apartment.

By this time, I was very frustrated with the whole

idea of the big city. I called Jack and told him the story of wanting to land a job on my own. He asked where I went, and when I said downtown, he just laughed and said if I wanted to find a job, he would help me find something closer to home. Coming from a small town, I thought downtown was where all the office jobs were located. Little did I know that in Milwaukee, there were offices everywhere and plenty of jobs for someone like me with good secretarial skills.

In November 1960, I was working as a private secretary for the sales manager of a family-owned company on Port Washington Road, not too far from where I lived. I took the car most days, and when the weather was inclement; my husband would drop me off and pick me up. Life was good.

1961

I got a call from home that my Dad had a heart attack. They rushed him to the hospital, and we learned that they couldn't do anything for him. The doctor suggested that he quit work and take care of himself. This must have been a real blow to our family because there were still eight children at home to care for.

The family agreed that Mom would go back to work. Before her childbearing years, Mom was an executive secretary and took pride in her work. She ended up going back to the same place she had previously worked. She had a good job, and she did a good job. Dad managed to keep the home fires intact. He was a wonderful cook. It seemed to work out well for the family. The doctors managed to put our dad on medication, and he lived almost twenty more years.

The last thing on my mind when I got married was starting a family. Being a staunch Catholic, I had only one method to prevent pregnancy: the rhythm method. One had to be very aware of her cycle. By late February, I realized I hadn't paid much attention to the calendar, and according to the doctor; my baby was due in November, 1961.

I didn't wait more than three months before giving my notice at work and spent the next few months knitting baby clothes and preparing for yet another move in order to have another bedroom for the baby.

We moved a few apartments away on the same street. We were a few doors closer to Capitol Drive and a few steps closer to Jack's work. The move went very well because we had not accumulated too much in a year.

The most exciting part of our move to a larger apartment was that I met a girl across the hall who was not only from my hometown, but who was also expecting her first baby. When we found out that we were both expecting in November, we immediately became good friends. Our husbands got along very well, too, and we ended up doing many things together before and after our babies were born. I went into the hospital one day before my new friend Pat, and we brought our new babies home on the same day.

CHAPTER 7

THE RYAN CHILDREN

JULIE ROCHELLE RYAN—
NOVEMBER 27, 1961

JULIE was a tiny one, weighing only six pounds, six ounces. It was so much fun being a first-time mom. I played house on a daily basis. My neighbor and I compared notes about our babies, Julie and Paula. Together, we watched them grow up those first few months. I loved apartment living in those early years.

Our new neighbors, Linda and Frank, were just as much fun, and Frank worked at the same place as Jack. Linda was a stay-at-home mom, too. Life was good! I had so much fun taking care of Julie and visiting with other moms and their babies. The days went by very fast. We lived just down the street from Estabrook Park, and we took our babies there almost every day.

Julie was a good baby, and I took her for many walks in the buggy. When she graduated to the stroller, I used to take her to the bus stop, fold up the stroller, hop on the bus, and go to Capitol Court to the shopping center. I would parade around the stores with little Julie. She looked like Pebbles from the Flintstones. I had her hair up in a top knot. I loved to hear the comments from the little old ladies. "Oh my! How cute!"

Sometimes, we'd be away half of the day just browsing through the big city stores. We did this on a regular basis. I'd usually get off the bus about a mile or more away from our apartment, and we would enjoy our walk home. I had Julie to myself for nearly three years and never even thought of going back to work. I loved being a mama.

In 1962, a man taking a survey knocked on my apartment door. The city wanted to see how many people felt the need for freeways. I remember telling him that it didn't matter to my family because my husband's office was right down the road, and he often walked to work. The guy just chuckled and left. Not much time passed before the freeways took over the city.

Linda asked me to be her sponsor for Confirmation into the Catholic Church. We hit a lot of traffic on our way to the church. We were in an intersection, close to the church, when I noticed smoke coming from beneath the hood of my car. I turned on the hazard lights, and we got out of the car. We opened the hood and saw flames. I didn't panic, but I must have looked quite flustered. Someone called the fire department from a nearby business.

A man came with a car blanket and tried to extinguish the flames. The fire seemed to be getting out of hand, but the fire department arrived, and with one spray of foam, the fire was out.

I often wanted to thank that man who stopped and

ruined his nice car blanket while trying to put out that fire. I did place a note of thanks to that unknown man in the Milwaukee Journal. I believe that there truly are angels in our midst, and he was one of those angels.

Not too long after the car fire, a scary thing happened one day while we lived in that upstairs apartment. My young brother, Chip, was staying with us for a few days. We had a small gas stove with a ledge by the back wall where I used to set the match box. I was sweeping the kitchen floor when the box of matches fell behind the stove and ignited. Chip and I moved fast. He tried to extinguish the fire while I ran to get little Julie off the potty seat.

In my haste, I could not unfasten the lap strap, so I took the whole seat—her still sitting on it—and we all ran to tell the neighbors of the fire.

Someone called the fire department, and soon there were sirens and fire trucks pulling up to the apartment building. I was holding Julie, simultaneously crying and laughing at how she looked with her little bare butt showing through the potty seat.

A fireman came up to me, and the first thing he said after he confirmed that I dwelled in the apartment was, "You did the right thing by calling the fire department." He said it was all clear to go back into the apartment and advised me to find a new place to keep the match box.

I wasn't ready for another child and thought I'd be

happy with just our Julie. God had another plan, and nearly three years later, we had Johnny.

JOHN MICHAEL RYAN, JR.—
AUGUST 22, 1964

This birth was a memorable event. I thought I was due in late August, but the doctor moved my due date up to the end of July. Therefore, anytime after mid-July, I was ready.

Patti and her husband, Bill, came to get Julie for a vacation up north. Surely, by the time she came home, there would be a sister waiting for her.

I was told all through my pregnancy that I was carrying another girl. Everything was the same as my previous pregnancy. Her name was going to be Jennifer Catherine; Jennifer, because we liked that name, and Catherine, after my mother.

Julie was back home and still had no sibling. One night, I thought the time had come. We called our friends who lived in the next block, and they came in the middle of the night to get Julie. By morning, I was back home because my labor had stopped. After this happened, my mother said not to worry. She came to Milwaukee with my sister, Jeanne, to take Julie home with her. I was glad little Jeanne needed a haircut because at least Mom's trip was not all for me. I remember cutting Jeanne's hair, barely being able to get close enough to her to get the job done.

On Friday night, I enjoyed several blueberry pancakes, dripping in maple syrup. On Saturday morning, I went for a checkup with Dr. Linn, he told me to head right over to St. Mary's Hospital on the lakefront. He would meet me there and induce labor. I was so ready to get this ordeal over with and take Jennifer home. The doctor broke my water, and they gave me a hypo to relax a little. The doctor left the hospital, and Jack went home.

Within an hour, they had me in the delivery room. The doctor rushed over, and my husband made it back on time. There were a couple of student nurses in the delivery room to experience their first delivery. Well, honey, it was a cakewalk. No pushing, no nothing. Out *he* came. Dr. Linn said, "What a cute little gir—Oh! It's a boy!" I'll never forget that. We had not picked out any boys' names but immediately decided his name would be John, after his dad and Dr. John Linn. How exciting! Now we had a boy and a girl.

Johnny weighed seven pounds, fifteen ounces, and slept all the time. My girlfriends would come over to see Johnny, and he was always sleeping. Perhaps I was settled down a little too, this being my second child, but I have to say he was a good baby. I guess they say the bigger the baby, the more they can consume at feeding time, and therefore, the more they sleep. Well, that was our Johnny! Julie loved helping me with the baby. She was so attentive to him, and I'd always let her help by handing me diaper pins when I needed to change her little brother.

I'd take both babies in the buggy and go for long walks. Even though Humboldt Avenue was a busy street, it was a pleasant neighborhood, and we enjoyed our walks. When Johnny graduated to the stroller, I'd put both of them in it, and on the bus we'd go for more adventures.

When Julie was four years old, the three of us went

shopping at Gimbles. I had Julie's hand, but she let go and got on the elevator before I was ready to put the stroller in with Johnny. Oh, my goodness! The door closed and the elevator went up. I'll never forget the nice man who helped me take the stairs so we could retrieve Julie on the next floor. I believe there were only two or three stories to the building. Needless to say, I was very happy to see Julie. She acted like nothing was wrong.

CHAPTER 8

OUR NEW HOME—1965

WITH two toddlers, we looked for a neighborhood where traffic would be quieter, and we located a duplex in the same neighborhood in which the mayor of Milwaukee lived. We celebrated Johnny's first birthday there, but we only stayed in the duplex for about six months.

We ended up building our dream home in the area of the Milwaukee Polo Field and the Melody Top. It was a new subdivision and afforded us a nice life. The tot park across the street was perfect for the kids and me to swing. I never seemed to let go of swinging. I spent untold hours with younger brothers and sisters in our neighborhood park in Menasha, and I'll love the swings forever.

Wall-to-wall carpet was the rage in the early sixties. I decided to return to work for the summer so we could afford to have our new home carpeted throughout. Lucky for us, my youngest sister, Colleen, came to help us out with the children. We covered those beautiful, completely finished hardwood floors with celery green carpet.

I'll bet the people who bought our house some years later had a ball ripping out that carpet and enjoying those hardwood floors. In the late sixties, plywood floors were covered with carpet in newly built homes. Installing carpet cost much less than installing hardwood floors.

Julie, Johnny, and I took frequent walks over to the Milwaukee Polo Field, which was right in our neighborhood. One day, we climbed to the very top of the bleachers. We pretended to watch a polo game, and cheered for our imaginary polo ponies. It was such a fun day. The next day, little Julie came up to me and said, "Mommy, can we go back over to those, um, you know … those washers again?" She couldn't think of the name "bleachers," but she connected it to the washing machine.

The three of us walked over to the Melody Top (a big tent-theater in the round) one afternoon and nobody was around, however, the big tent was open. We went in and walked down to the cement stage floor. While we were pretending to be acting, a man's voice echoed through the theater. "Hey, what are you doing in here?" He laughed with us as we told him we lived in the neighborhood and were just pretending to be acting in a play. We humbly made our exit.

We had a lot of fun with our family of four. We took pictures of the children for our Christmas cards, pictures of them at the park, and pictures of all of us at the zoo. Pictures, pictures, pictures everywhere. We had everything we wanted, and everyone was in good health.

Oh yes, the children afforded many hours of contentment and fun for all of us. We were the perfect family with the perfect children, in the perfect new subdivision, in the perfect new house. We worked like dogs creating a nice lawn and planting shrubs and a garden, and we even had a pool installed in our backyard. We were very happy.

I used to make clothes for myself and would make little dresses for Julie that matched. I dressed John with white shirts, little sport jackets, and bow ties for church. I wore hats and white gloves and high heels, and my husband always dressed in a suit, white shirt, and tie. We glowed! We were on top of the world! Or were we?

Before I go any further, I must say how critical I was of anyone going through problems with their spouses. Divorce was a no-no, and I was glad that there was no way that I would ever have to worry about that.

I belonged to a ladies' neighborhood group. We met once a month at someone's house. We would either play cards or knit or do whatever the hostess had planned for the evening. I don't recall anyone saying nice things about their husbands, but all I could do was brag about mine. I never ran him down. He had a good job, he was a good provider, and he was a good husband and father. We went to church every Sunday, and the four of us would get compliments about what a nice little family we were.

PART II

CHAPTER 9

SOMETHING HAPPENED!

I am not ashamed of the fact that by 1965, I desperately wanted to get an office job. Though Jack was greatly opposed to this, eventually he gave in. In my absence, one of my neighbor ladies took good care of the children.

I was very good at typing and shorthand and ended up being a private secretary to the sales manager of a fine company in Milwaukee. I loved my new job. I worked hard and felt highly fulfilled with family, household chores, and a full-time job. Even though Jack said I didn't have to work, I wanted to exercise my secretarial skills and save some money of my own.

The day that I was supposed to start my new job, I had to call my boss and inform him that both of my children had come down with chicken pox and I would have to stay with them for another week. They were very understanding and held my position until I could leave the children in a neighbor's care and go to work. By the time that confinement was over, I was overjoyed to get out of the house.

While at work, I found that there was only one person that I could totally relate to. His name was Wally, and he was separated from his wife and family. He was staying with an aunt and uncle in Milwaukee. I felt sorry for him and found myself trying to be an attentive friend that he could talk to. He had a good position and did his work well.

We used to walk across the street to the popular bowling alley for lunch every day while others would open their brown bag lunches at their desks. We laughed at the way the rest of the office staff spent their lunch break— anything to cover up for the feelings that were growing between us. I grew very fond of Wally. He came from a simple family.

His father had died while ten-year-old Wally was with him on a business trip. Wally was unable to wake his father. While at a hotel in a strange town, Wally went to the front desk and said, "I can't wake my Dad." His father, in his late forties, had died of a massive heart attack.

Wally grew very close to his mother, and instead of after-school sports, he worked at paper routes and odd jobs in order to help his mom.

Over the months, Wally and I often shared our thoughts and feelings, and we grew closer and closer. Meanwhile, my husband was moving up the corporate ladder so fast I could hardly keep up with him. I know I should have appreciated my husband's achievements; however, looking back, I think I was trying to justify my own emotions.

Jack and I were at the Pfister Hotel in Milwaukee for a function with the company Jack worked for. I realized that I did not want to be there. I started wondering what I really wanted in life.

I was so proud of being able to make nice things for myself. I had made my Muskrat jacket in fur class, and I had also made my yellow brocade dress. However, at these functions, I felt very inferior to my husband's coworkers' wives, with their huge diamond rings and full-length mink coats.

I wanted a simple life where I could be happy. I didn't care about diamonds and furs. I still don't. I also didn't like that the cigar-smoking big guys kept promising my husband the world as long as he continued to do well with the company.

Business trips for Jack came more and more frequently, and I found myself alone with the children much of the time.

One Saturday, my husband went to watch a basketball star in the Chicago area with a friend. I told Wally that I was going to be alone that Saturday, and we ended up meeting at the bowling alley for an afternoon of bowling and fun with my two children. I invited him over for hamburgers afterward, and all was well. He left, and that was that.

Jack arrived home well after midnight that evening. I hadn't slept a wink and was feeling guilty for spending most of the afternoon with Wally, caring less that my husband was gone. I confessed to him that I was very fond of a coworker and felt that he, my husband, and I were growing apart. It seemed to me that he was spending more time with his business travels and his friends than with me and the children. Of course, I was trying to justify my feelings for someone else.

Needless to say, Jack was very unhappy with me. He made me quit my office job immediately. Though I disagreed, I knew it was best if I wanted to keep our family together. Jack called my boss and simply said that, due to problems at home, I would not be back in the office.

I tried very hard to be a stay-at-home wife to Jack and a good mother to my two lovely children.

A couple of weeks after I left my job, I phoned a coworker. She said they missed me. She was so nice to me. We chatted, but she never asked why I quit. I wanted so badly to find out how Wally was doing, but I just couldn't ask. Finally, before I hung up, I asked her how that nice tall fellow was doing, pretending I had forgotten his name. She mentioned a different Wally, but I said, "No, no, that tall one with the dark mustache." She said, "Well, he left shortly after you did." I was really sad then because I knew he lived out of town, and I would probably never hear from him again.

It was at this time that the Milwaukee riots took place. I had joined the Christ Child Society and had been going down to the inner core of the city every Monday to assist the children at St. Gall's School, now called Martin Luther King School. I gave extra care to a girl named Pam who seemed to like the attention, and her efforts warmed my heart.

Because of the unrest in Milwaukee, my dad was

adamant that I not go into the inner core anymore. The last time I went to the school, I experienced what I deemed to be my sign to stay away. I had to park several blocks from the school this particular day, and the hoodlums, as we called them, were speaking crudely and roughly to me. They wanted to know what I was doing down there with their kids.

I was glad to get back home that day and immediately called the nun in charge of my program. I told her I had to watch out for my safety in order to be able to care for my own children. It was so hard for me to leave St. Gall's, and I surely missed Pam.

Until we meet again, and we *will* meet again, Pam.

While I still really missed Wally, after losing my volunteer time at St. Gall's School, I was determined more than ever to pick up the pieces of my life and make the best of what I had. I did just that at the time. I tore apart bedrooms and completely redecorated and painted everything. I took my leisure time and made a life for my family. I was not truly happy, but it was the best I could do.

At this point in my life, I didn't really know how to pray to the Lord for help in this dreadful situation. I continued to try to fix everything by myself and actually dug the hole deeper.

Two years later, I was painting my daughter's bedroom and Jack was helping me. The phone rang. I answered. It was Wally. I was so proud of myself because I just hung up! I went back to painting and told my husband that I had just hung up on Wally. He didn't seem too concerned and just said, "Good for you." I was heartsick later that evening. I really wanted to know how Wally was doing.

When the phone rang the next afternoon, Wally said, "Please don't hang up." I didn't. We chatted for a long time, catching up on the last two years. He was now divorced. He said he just was wondering how I was doing. He said he had a meeting in Milwaukee the following week, so we agreed to meet at a restaurant for coffee. I knew I was okay, though, and thought it would be harmless just to meet, chat, and have coffee.

When we met, my heart flipped, and I realized I couldn't see him and not be involved with him.

Oh my goodness! This is hard to relive, but it is part of my story. One thing led to another, and my husband and I decided to separate and try to sort things out. I felt relieved because now I wouldn't have to answer to him.

I worked hard at being attentive to my children, keeping up the house and yard, and staying in touch with Wally. Even though he was divorced, he had a family to support. He had a nice job back in his hometown, which was about an hour away from Milwaukee.

Wally would drive one hour almost every night after work to spend the supper hour with me and the children, and then he would drive an hour to get back home. I was thrilled with the attention, and it prompted me to once again make nice meals for the children.

My Dad knew what was going on, and he let me know

in no uncertain terms that he would absolutely not even think about another person in my life. He told me, and justifiably so, "If you feel you have to divorce your husband, fine, but don't bring anyone else to my doorstep."

During this time in the late sixties, when Julie was in fourth grade and Johnny in second, Wally asked me if I would move to his hometown area in Eden. He found a little house for me and spent a lot of time fixing it up and painting it to my specifications, and once school was out, the children and I made our move to Eden. The children made some friends in the neighborhood, and Wally's family included the children and me in their family functions.

The school was close enough to see from our house, so the kids could walk there. I helped out at the school during lunchtime. Between that and keeping busy decorating and rearranging my house, I kept pretty busy. I loved the little town of Eden. It seemed like we lived in the country—we could hear and see the cows in the distance. The neighbors were nice to me, and some of our friends from Milwaukee would occasionally arrive for a visit.

This is the time in my life that I felt Julie and Johnny brought me up! They were so good about just going along with whatever I thought was best. They seemed happy; I still was not. I didn' know why, but I just was not content. I didn't know how to pray for help. I kept trying to fix things on my own.

After I had lived in Eden for about nine months, Wally and I had a falling out. The next day he was going to be in a golf tournament all day, and Jack was going to pick up the kids and take them to the park. When Jack arrived, I was in tears. He invited me to spend the day with them. I did.

Before noon that day, I had made up my mind to move back to Milwaukee and into the house with Jack. By that time, I was mentally such a mess that I figured it just didn't matter.

Jack went back to Milwaukee to get a neighbor to help him move me back, and they returned with a U-Haul. In the meantime, I called my Dad to tell him what was going on. An hour or so later, in walked my Dad, my sister Patti, and my brother Jim. They had come to help me pack. By the end of the day, the kids and I were on our way back to Milwaukee.

When Wally went over to my house in Eden the next day, he found the Thunderbird that he had lent me in the driveway and an empty house. He was very upset, but after phoning me and finding out that I was trying to take care of myself, he agreed that we should part ways. I imagine that Wally was happy to get rid of me.

Again, I uprooted the children. Though my friends welcomed us back, they knew I was a mental mess.

CHAPTER 10

TROUBLED WATERS— FALL OF 1970

IT was another very hot fall day. Julie, age nine and Johnny, age six, were off to school. I stood in the door, tweezing my eyebrows as I watched them board the bus. As soon as they were gone, I literally collapsed in tears by the kitchen table over a cup of coffee and a cigarette. I didn't know where my life was going. I was unhappy in my marriage and found myself struggling each day to survive. I had made such a mess of everything. I wondered what the next step would be. My weekly visits to my psychiatrist didn't seem to be enough.

Julie and John were too young to get involved in a divorce, but that is where my husband and I seemed to be headed. I didn't want to put the children through the trials of a divorce. I always felt sorry for the children of divorced families. "Oh well," I thought, "this will pass." I glanced at the clock and realized that I had only a few minutes to get myself ready for school. I dried my eyes and tried to make some sense out of my day. My class would begin in an hour, and it was at the other end of town.

I had signed up for beautician school. This was something I had always wanted to do; I enjoyed cutting hair and working with wig styling. Jack did not want me to work, but I felt compelled to keep busy outside of the home when everyone else was away during the daytime hours.

That particular morning, I hurried to get ready, brushed up on my lesson, and had another cup of coffee and another cigarette. I thought that I should really call my psychiatrist and tell him what a bad day I was having, but it was only 8:00 AM. "No, not now," I thought. "Perhaps I would do that later, when I get back home."

I arrived at school. I had made many friends and once again, I pretended that nothing was wrong. I chatted with friends before class, laughed and shared what we had studied, or in my case, what I hadn't. I was thirty-one years old and one of the oldest in the class. It really didn't bother me. It was fun to mother them and give them advice when they asked.

All day, I kept looking at the clock. I didn't want to be there, but I didn't want to return home; I just didn't want to be anywhere. I was restless, and I knew I didn't have the perfect life. I was living two lives: the one my friends knew and the one I knew.

I finally got home after school. It was very hot and muggy; we didn't have air conditioning. The children seemed irritable. Jack seemed irritable. I was miserable. I had a glass of wine before dinner to try to relax. I was not up to cooking, so I put out some leftovers. I couldn't eat—I didn't want to eat. I was down to one hundred and ten pounds and was never hungry anymore.

The children retired just after dark. Jack was watching Monday Night Football. I was feeling so detached, like I was being sucked into hell. I just couldn't cope any longer.

I didn't want to call my psychiatrist because he would think I was going crazy. After all, when I did see him, I really hadn't been very honest. I was only going to him because Jack wanted me to. I was seeing him once a week, and that should have been enough. I decided against calling him because I had an appointment with him later that week.

I told Jack that I was going to retire early that evening and that I didn't want him to wake me after I got to sleep, so I asked him to sleep on the couch. I went to bed and just laid there and cried. I went in to talk to Julie, but I found that she was asleep. I peeked in on Johnny, age four, but he, too, was sound asleep. I didn't want to talk to Jack. Who could I talk to? My neighborhood friends, Kay and Ginny, lived very close, but again, I didn't want anyone to know that I had a problem. The other neighbors were all busy with their own families.

Maybe I should call Dad. No, maybe I should call Mom because she seems to understand things better than Dad. But Dad was not in very good health, and Mom was working full-time, plus they had all the other children to care for. I just wanted to spare everyone my troubles. Somehow, I thought I would get through the night.

I went back to bed and turned out the light. Maybe I would get so tired from crying that I would just fall asleep. Sleep did not come. I had a terrible headache. I couldn't stand it any longer. I needed to do something to take away the pain. I didn't give it another thought.

Suicide never entered my mind. I simply went into the bathroom and took my antidepressant medication; I swallowed every last pill. I followed this with aspirin, whatever was left in the bottle. I grabbed my rosary, went into Julie's room, and kissed her goodnight on the forehead, and I did the same with Johnny.

I would be completely at peace soon. I felt better already. I tucked myself safely into the middle of the bed and covered myself and started to say the rosary. I knew that when I woke, I would be with God and I wouldn't have anymore problems.

God had a different plan for me. I managed to fall out of bed. Jack called the paramedics. I remember that they asked me if I took any pills. They asked for the bottles. Though I had hidden them, I walked right to them and turned the empty bottles over.

The next recollection I have was when I woke up the next morning in the hospital. I called for the nurse. Then, a group of doctors came in and talked to me and made me realize that I had almost taken my own life. "I'm sorry," I said. It was foolish, and I vowed to never do anything like that again. I just wanted to go home. I looked for my purse, but it was not there. I looked for my clothes, but the nurse said that all I had on when I arrived were my pajamas, slippers, and a coat. I needed a tooth brush and a comb, but I didn't have any.

I called Jack at home, but there was no answer. Where was everyone? Oh, I thought, he was probably at the office. The children were probably in school. I called him at the office. He was very compassionate but was also very upset with me. Justifiably so. Now what? I promised to never do anything like that again, and he came to pick me up. Before the hospital released me, I promised that I would seek more therapy and possibly in-house treatment if I could not get beyond my issues.

Neither of us said a word the whole way home. I didn't know if or what he had told anyone, and I didn't ask. Julie and John didn't say anything when they got home from school. Nobody called. The evening was quiet; I was scared.

I hurt all over. The paramedics must have pounded my chest hard to keep my heart beating. I felt like they had broken my ribs. I had a severe headache, too. I couldn't even think of eating. Just the thought of food made me ill. I had lost another couple of pounds, and I felt very weak. I went to bed early. I had a fitful night, and sleep came sporadically.

I was bound and determined to go to school. I forced myself out of bed in the morning and saw the children off to school. I was having a very hard time getting going. The temperature was in the mid-nineties again, and I looked ridiculous in a sweater. I needed it to cover all of the needle marks and bruises on my arms from the intravenous feedings and shots that I was given in the hospital.

When I arrived at school, several people asked why I was wearing a sweater. I told them that I was not feeling well that day. I got through the day but didn't have a clue what the teacher was talking about, nor did I care. I had to quit school for lack of concentration. So be it. I just didn't care anymore.

My husband covered nicely for me at beautician school, simply telling them that we were having some family problems which must be dealt with and I would no longer be attending class. They promptly refunded a certain percentage of my fees, which helped greatly with my negative attitude at this point in my life. People really did care. Complete strangers were so nice to me and just wanted to help me. They told my husband to tell me that I would be missed and to let them know if I ever wanted to go back. This meant so much to me. It proved to me that people really can make a difference when the chips are down.

The evening hours of that awful day dragged on, and I finally called my Dad and told him just how I was feeling. He nicely encouraged me to take care of myself and enter into a treatment center to get some help. I had never heard him so calm. I knew he was concerned for me. I am sure this was very difficult for Mom and Dad. Dad talked to Jack for a few minutes, and I felt I was starting to settle down a little.

The next day, my mother and sister Patti came to Milwaukee to help my husband with the decision of admitting me to a facility in Wauwatosa, Wisconsin, where I would get some help. When they were in the kitchen planning things for me; I was in the living room, lying on the couch and just crying my heart out. I was so afraid!

When the facility admitted me, I had to agree to stay there for at least five weeks. I had hit rock bottom, and I knew I needed help to sort out my life. God had a different plan for me, but back then, I didn't know it, and I didn't really know Him.

CHAPTER 11

HOSPITALIZED FOR
FIVE WEEKS

EVERYONE at the facility was very nice to me, especially other patients. Some of them even hugged me and assured me I would get better. This helped me stay calm and put my mind to rest. The people there told me not to even think about the world outside and to just concentrate on getting stronger in my mind so that I would be ready to make decisions when it came time for me to leave.

I kept thinking about my Dad. I still wanted to please him and hoped that at some point, I would take charge of my life and make my own decisions. This bothered me a lot, but I told the therapist about it, and the people at the facility helped me work through it. I did what I was told, and I finally put my Dad out of my mind and listened to my therapist.

When I entered the facility, I had to surrender all of the personal items that could possibly enable me to harm myself. This included my razor, hair spray, nail scissors, aspirin, and the like. I weighed the least I ever had in my

adult life, and my light weight completely sapped the
energy that I would need in order to pick up the pieces of
my life. The facility took care of this immediately; the staff
monitored my eating and gave me prescription medica-
tions—that they watched me take—in order to increase
my appetite. The food was appealing, and I found myself
looking forward to all of the meals.

In these next few paragraphs, I will try to recall some
of the reasons the other patients were in treatment. I will
do this in order to show just how sane I was and how much
I had going for me compared to other people. That was an
immediate eye-opener for me; I realized how much I had
been blessed in life. I had a wonderful husband, two fine
children, and a new home in the outskirts of Milwaukee.
What more could I possibly want? This was the trump card
that I needed most. Though I never wanted to feel better
at someone else's expense, doing so helped me realize that I
had a healthy mind and that my problems could be solved
once I became strong again.

People enter into facilities like the one I was in for a
number of reasons. One person, whom I will call Phil,
was there because he felt no self worth at all. He had tried
to commit suicide a few times, but to no avail. He had
tried drugs, but they only left him with addiction. Alcohol
didn't appeal to him. We never discussed his faith, which,
by the way, was not number one in my mind at that point
of my life. Hindsight shows me that this is what I was
lacking most in my life.

I had never seen depression in a male, before, and

I was sad for him. He was such a nice-looking man, so polite and helpful to others. He had been there for about three weeks already, and I guess what he was learning was really helping him. Long story short, the day that Phil left Admissions, a locked unit where you may not have visitors or phone calls until they are well enough to move to another building, was the day that I felt there was hope for me. He had grown so much stronger in his mind. He started making plans for when he would leave the facility. He started smiling and helping others more instead of being so sad and withdrawn.

I don't know what ever happened to Phil, but I do know that he helped me to get stronger in my mind, and eventually, I, too, was able to leave Admissions and move to another building where I had the freedom to take walks on my own. I could even make some phone calls.

I felt myself getting stronger every day, and I was zeroing in on the positives of my life and letting go of the negatives.

My husband and children came to visit me often. I saw a psychiatrist every day, except for the weekends. One weekend, I was actually allowed to go home for a few hours. I felt like a fish out of water and couldn't wait until I got back to the safety of the facility. I knew, then, that therapy was helping me. I knew why I was required to stay there the full five weeks.

When my time was up, they gave me the option of going home permanently with the knowledge that if I needed to go back, they would be there for me.

There was only one thing I had to do before they would release me. I had to call my Dad and tell him that no matter what, I had to make my own decisions about my future, and I had to remain strong in those decisions and take whatever consequences life dealt me. For the first time in my entire life, my Dad agreed with me. He admitted that he was too controlling and that in the future, he would not meddle in my life, but he would always be there for me if I needed him.

After five weeks, I had learned a lot and felt I was ready to get on with life and make a life for myself and my children. Though I had a long way to go, I put those past five weeks into my memory and hoped they would stay with me and nourish me for the rest of my life. They have.

Though I call this "The Storm" in my life, it was also a learning experience, and it toughened me up in order to get through other trying times. It also has afforded me a great respect for mental health professionals. From that time on, I have always encouraged people to seek professional help if needed, and, even more importantly, to develop a personal relationship with God.

CHAPTER 12

HANGING IN THERE FOR THE KIDS' SAKE

JACK and I tried to stay together for the children's sake. I was not happy with him, and he couldn't have been happy with me. I found myself taking the advice of my therapist. I had to do the inevitable or end up back in the hospital. I had to make a decision and stick to it. I felt strong enough to make my decision at this point, knowing full well that I would have to go back to work—eventually full-time—buy my own car, and take care of the house and the children by myself. Though it was still somewhat difficult to bid my husband goodbye, we both knew we had given it a good try.

Wally was back into my life within a few months, and Jack seemed to be doing well with his girlfriend. Both Jack and I respected each others' choices, and we both had promised to always put the children first in our lives.

After the divorce, everyone seemed to settle down somewhat. Julie and John seemed to accept the situation, and Jack and I saw to our children's every need.

Eventually, Jack transferred to the Chicago area with

his company. He didn't want to leave Milwaukee because of the children, but we worked things out, and he saw them as much as possible. We finalized our divorce, and we dealt with the ramifications of that forever after. Divorce when children are involved is a never-ending struggle.

Life had its challenges. Wally knew much time would pass before things settled enough for us to get married. Still, that was our goal. There was no turning back.

I was allowed to stay in the house until I remarried. This worked out okay. Wally was well aware that I was raising two children, and our house rules would not permit him to live with us. He was fine with that. He found himself a job in Milwaukee, rented an apartment in Wauwatosa, and we went about our daily lives.

I found a part-time job as a secretary to the proprietor of a well-known florist. I worked from 9:00 AM until 2:00 PM, five days a week. Soon, I realized that I was doing eight hours of work in a five hour day. The children were both in school, and I felt it was the time to secure a full-time position with benefits.

In 1973, I read an ad in the Milwaukee Journal seeking an executive secretary to the president and owner of a tropical plant rental place in the neighborhood where I lived. The business was also just around the corner from the kids' school. Even though I had never considered myself to an executive secretary, I applied for that job. I called my Dad. He cheered me on and wished me well.

It was a long week before I heard from my boss-to-be, Mr. Allis, again. He called me in for a second interview after he checked with the company with which I was currently employed. Mr. Allis told me that my current boss said, "If you hire Suzanne, you will be adding another flower to your shop." What a compliment! I was ecstatic and accepted the full-time position. I started out at six hundred dollars per month with regular compensation as the years went by.

Julie was twelve, and John was nine. My new job worked out very well because if the children missed their bus, they would walk to my office and do their homework while waiting for me. They were extremely good kids, and I never had to worry about them being alone after school.

Summer time was a little more of a challenge because Julie was going to be taking care of John, but because I was right around the corner, I knew it would be okay. We lived on a dead end street, and just across the way sat a park that kept them occupied on a daily basis. We had a swimming pool in our back yard, but they had explicit orders not to even think about the pool until I got home.

One hot summer day, I got a call from Julie. She told me that John was acting up and asked me what she should do. I said "I'll be right there." I told my boss I'd be right back. I surprised Johnny when I came on the scene. He never acted up again. When I got back to the office not more than ten minutes later, my boss said, "I really respect you for that. You put your family first."

I did a fine job for this company. When my boss sold the company in 1980, the new owner's accountant worked on our books for days. He told my boss that he had never seen such accurate records, and my boss passed that on to me. I took pride in that job, and to this day I refer to it as "The Big Job," and I still refer to Mr. Allis as "my boss."

Julie and John loved Wally, and that helped immensely.

They all got along so well, and Wally knew I was the primary parent and he never interfered. There was a place called Hoffman's Glass Rainbow Cocktail Lounge & Restaurant located just around the corner from my house. I used to groom Julie for babysitting. Once in awhile, I would put dinner in the oven and meet Wally for a glass of wine at the lounge, a test to see how the kids would do. We were just two minutes away. Wally ate supper with us almost every night.

My neighbors liked Wally a lot, too, and periodically, we were invited to someone's house for cards. We laughed about this years later, but one very foggy night, Wally stayed at my neighbor's house so he didn't have to drive home in the fog. Not too long after that, he would spend the night on my couch if situations prevented him from driving home.

Wally had accepted a job downtown at an executive placement service, thinking he might find the perfect job by doing this. He did. I don't mind giving the name of this company. He worked for Dick Yoder, the owner of Allied Pools in Milwaukee, Appleton, and Green Bay. Wally finally found what suited him best. He made an excellent salesman, and his sales slips proved it. When he received his first paycheck from Allied, he came over to my house and waved that check in my face and had tears in his eyes. He was sure that it was going to be temporary, but little did he know, the job was perfect for him. He had this "Wally way" about him and was not a high pressure salesman at all. He excelled with this company and for this company, and in 1988, he became the company's only Million Dollar Salesman.

CHAPTER 13

ENGAGEMENT TO WALLY

WALLY'S boss, Dick, took good care of his employees. We were both very excited about Wally's position with Allied. Within a few months, we got engaged, feeling that things were finally picking up for us, and we felt comfortable looking ahead and not dwelling on the rocky past. We had no wedding date planned. We were just happy to make the commitment to each other.

Sometimes, it seemed impossible that we that could get married. I was Catholic, had not gotten an annulment, and had no intentions of leaving the Church. Somehow, though, I knew that even though people would turn me away, I knew that God would not. I knew my heart was in the right place. Though I did not go to the Catholic Church in my neighborhood for fear that people would talk; I did attend a Catholic Church every Sunday. Wally went with me on a regular basis.

When Jack was in town, he would pick up the children for Church and spend the day with them. I was grateful that he stayed in their lives. They liked spending time with their dad. He was back in his relationship with his friend, and I was glad that we were both content, finally.

Wally and I were at a Catholic Church in Milwaukee one Sunday. An usher came up to us and tapped Wally on the shoulder and asked if the two of us would like to take the gifts up (gifts consisted of the chalice of wine and communion wafers). Wally looked quizzically at me, and I simply said, "We don't belong to this parish." The usher nicely said, "It doesn't matter, would you take the gifts up?" At that point, I decided this was like God tapping Wally on the shoulder and saying, "It doesn't matter, just do it!" I said, "Yes, we would," and we both walked up with the gifts at the proper time. I can't tell you what this meant to me. At this moment I thought, "You know, people may turn you away, but God sure won't."

We both were more comfortable in church after that and attended regularly. Even though by church rules, as a divorcee, I was not supposed to receive communion again, I figured God would never turn me away, and I continued to receive and pray for guidance and forgiveness.

Wally used to stay in the pew when I went to communion. I never urged him to receive, but I made it clear that when he felt the time was right, he should join me. At midnight Mass on Christmas Eve in 1973, he let me into the aisle and suddenly I felt his hands, folded in prayer, nudge me in the back. I turned around, and he smiled at me and continued forward to receive communion. I felt that this was another sign that God was guiding both of us. I shed a few tears during that service, and Wally was emotional, too.

Dad still didn't want to meet Wally, but Dad and I stayed in touch on a regular basis. Occasionally, Julie, John, and I would go to The Valley for an overnight stay at

Mom and Dad's. Wally's name never came up. Dad knew we were still together, but he didn't want to hear about it.

One time, we were all invited to my sister Kathy's house in Neenah. Kathy and Ted had already met Wally, and they welcomed him into their home. While we were there, Dad called, and my young niece, Sara, answered the phone. Dad said "What are you doing, babe?" He always called Sara "babe." She said. "Oh, we're playing cards with Aunt Sue and Uncle Wally." Oh yikes! We all just looked at each other and held our breath (while we snickered). Little Sara was oblivious to any of the details of "Uncle Wally" and his lack of an invitation into her grandpa's life.

In January, 1974 my two-year-old nephew, Scott Laemmrich (Patti and Bill's son), was diagnosed with leukemia. This took over our family's emotions completely. Even our Dad became noticeably more tranquil. We all felt the trauma that the Laemmrich family was experiencing. They had to admit Scotty to the University of Minnesota Hospital where he was treated with tender, loving care. These events shook me so much that I decided to take a week off and fly to Minneapolis to spend some time with my sister, her husband, and little Scotty. This was such a sad time for all of us.

While I was in their room one evening, the phone rang. Patti answered it, and it was Dad, checking up on Scotty and chatting with Patti. Dad knew I was there, and before they hung up, he asked to talk to me.

This conversation turned out to be a turning point in my situation. Dad said he felt that it was time to meet Wally. He thought it was nice that Wally would stay with the children and afford me the time to spend with Patti in her time of need. My heart skipped beats during this phone conversation. This was a huge thing for our dad to do. He said that he and Mom would be home on Easter Sunday, and he knew that Wally was going to drive to Minneapolis to pick me up. He asked if we would mind driving a little out of our way to stop at their house in Menasha so he and Mom could meet Wally.

Dad seemed to realize the fragility of life. I knew that Wally, being the kind of forgiving person he was, would not hesitate to go out of his way to meet my Dad.

The Easter Sunday of 1974 produced a huge spring snowstorm. We were driving on Interstate 94 in the blinding snow. We stopped at a restaurant for lunch, and it was sad to see that the place was empty except for mounds of food.

We decided we could not get off of the interstate and wrestle with the storm on country roads. We could not go to Menasha. I went to the phone booth and called Dad to tell him we couldn't make it and hoped that he would ask us another time. He answered the phone and was so glad to hear from me. He said he was praying that we would get home safely, and he hoped we would make a trip to Menasha soon. We went the next weekend.

When my Dad met Wally, he immediately checked out Wally's shoes. He always told us girls in our dating years to "check out their shoes—if their shoes are neat and polished, it says a lot about the man." After he checked out Wally's shoes, he looked at me and winked. I knew he had approved of Wally.

Everything seemed to progress nicely. Wally and I were very happy together and the children seemed to approve of our relationship. Soon the children were in their pre-teens and all eyes were on their accomplishments.

Julie proved challenging during her teenage years; however, as I look back, I can see why she became a little obstinate as she approached her teens.

She attended Dominican High School in Whitefish Bay. One of the reasons I loved to go to their basketball games was because my Frederick Street neighbor, Don Gosz, was their coach. Dominican was in the middle of their second undefeated season. I had a pair of zebra-stripped corduroy pants. Julie didn't like them. That particular night, I walked into the gym with those pants on. Julie's girlfriends didn't know I was Julie's Mom and one of them said "Oh my gosh! Look at that lady's pants!" Julie just looked and never admitted to her friends that it was her mom, until I spotted her and started waving and shouting "Hi Julie!

Julie hung around with some really nice girls who lived on Milwaukee's lakefront in those big houses. One New Year's Eve, she was going to a sit-down dinner party at one of their homes. When I saw her in blue jeans, I hit the roof. I insisted that she wear something nicer for the party. She promptly called her girlfriend Terry, took her suitcase, and when Terry picked her up, away they went. I saw them driving around and around the block for awhile. Pretty soon, she stormed into the house and pretended to be changing her clothes.

John had a friend over to play games that night, and Wally and I went to a neighbor's for New Year's Eve dinner. When we got home, John couldn't wait to tell us that Julie went to the party in her blue jeans.

Apparently, she thought she would be home before me. Those were the silly little things that I would get so upset about with the kids. Hindsight tells me that those little things just didn't matter. They were good kids.

We didn't have to impose a curfew on the children while we lived in Milwaukee because when 10:00 PM came, if they were under eighteen, they had to be home. There was a notice at 10:00 PM on television every night that said, "Parents, do you know where your children are?" (Some parents heard "Children, Do you know where your parents are?)

When they turned eighteen, I figured they were responsible young adults with good judgment, and I wanted them to have the privileges of being out late and using good judgment.

I only remember one time when Julie's bad judgment card trumped her good judgment card. She took her car and went out with some girls. I never worried and liked the fact that she was the driver. I knew her. I trusted her.

One night, I got a call from Julie's girlfriend at one o' clock in the morning. Her friend, Jackie, called me "Mrs." because she couldn't remember my name. She said, "Mrs., um, Julie isn't feeling too well, so she is going to stay at my house overnight." Naturally, I was upset. I didn't know she had been drinking until the next morning when she came moping into the house as white as a sheet.

Julie had a job at the same place that I worked, and she asked if I would call in sick for her. It was the day before Mother's Day, in a florist shop, so I went to work for her, telling her we would talk about it later. I was mad!

When I got to work, my boss's wife had gotten wind of

Julie's illness and what had caused it. She said, "Now, don't be too hard on her. Tell Julie that the first time I got sick at a beer party, I threw up in somebody's clothes chute." That line broke the ice, and when I got home, Julie and I had a nice talk. It left an impression on Julie, and we never faced a situation like that in the future.

John's teen years went by uneventfully. Both Wally and I were very involved in the children's sports at school.

Johnny was always by my side making sure I was okay. This happened as a result of my hospitalization in 1970, I am sure. One never knows what a negative impression can be made during adverse situations.

Johnny was playing with his pet hamster, Herman. Johnny had a little wooden garage sitting on the floor, and he would put Herman on top, and we had fun watching him slide down the roof. He did that time after time. It came time for the children to go to bed, so Johnny put Herman back in his cage, and all was quiet.

In the morning, Johnny said "Mommy, there are nine little pink things in Herman's cage." You guessed it; Herman had nine babies that night. Gosh! Poor Herman was in labor while sliding down Johnny's garage roof. We immediately changed Herman's name to Amy and started to plan for raising all of those hamsters.

Johnny's teacher said it would be okay to bring the hamsters to Show And Tell. Away went Amy in the cage with her nine babies. The wheel in the hamster cage went round and round constantly. It seemed like Amy was trying to get back in shape.

We didn't have too many takers for the hamsters as they grew to full size, but the store where we purchased the hamsters gladly accepted all the babies. Amy loved being an only child again.

Amy went missing for several days. We finally found her in the sump pump water, and that was the end of our beloved Amy.

As the children grew older and became responsible, I began to realize that they truly were the blessings in my life.

Johnny became John when he was in his early teens. I got a call from the pastor at St. Bernadette's one time, telling me that John was caught on the roof of the rectory. Apparently, he was retrieving a basketball that one of his friends had shot up there. I immediately took John up to meet the pastor and apologize. The pastor humbly accepted John's apology and told him to say The Lord's Prayer five times, followed by several rosaries.

In hindsight, this next incident wasn't so bad. However, with Milwaukee's curfew being 10:00 PM and John still not home, I became anxious.

John and his friend, Derik, had taken the city bus to Dominican High School for a night basketball game. He had bus money to return home, but the bus stopped running, and John and Derik decided to walk home. Eleven pm came, and I was a basket case. Julie was already home from the game, and though she had seen John at the game, she didn't know what happened to him.

I asked Wally to go and look for John. I wanted to stay back by the phone in case he called. Wally was driving down North 76th Street around half passed eleven in the evening when he heard, "Hey, Wally!" There were John and Derik, waving to Wally like nothing was wrong. They had missed the bus and decided to use their bus money to buy a soda and hot dog, and they were walking home. They had no idea what time it was.

When he got home, I hit the roof. He retreated to his room, and awhile later, I felt a little guilty that I was so hard on him. By this time, I was just relieved that he was okay. I went to his room and found him sitting on the edge of his bed, crying while he was reading his Bible. Oh my! That stirred my motherly instincts, and I tried to be more cautious in my parenting after that.

Like I said, there were times when my children brought me up. It was a very hot Sunday morning. I was floating in our swimming pool when sixteen-year-old John came to the back screen door. He said, "Mom, what time are we going to Church?" I said I had decided not to go because it was so hot, and I thought we could just have a little Bible study later. He said, "Okay, I'll take my bike." You never saw anyone move as fast as I did! Off to church we went.

Not long after Dad met Wally, we decided to set a wedding date. As usual, I wanted Dad's approval.

Dad was most gracious and said at this point he thought it would be best for all of us. He grew fond of Wally. Finally, the unhappiness of the early 1970s seemed far away.

CHAPTER 14

SUZANNE MEYER—
OCTOBER 30, 1976

WE were married in a Christian ceremony on October 30, 1976. Some dear friends of ours, Mae and Walter, had a reception at their home for us. It was lovely and if I only could have stopped crying (tears of happiness) for a little while, I might have enjoyed it more. Kaye and Charlie stood up for us and our good friend, Gene Brah walked me down the isle. It was an unbelievable event for Wally and me. We treasured every moment.

Between Jack and my neighbors, they all assured us that we could go on our honeymoon, and we wouldn't have to worry about the children. Julie was fifteen and John was twelve. They seemed to accept our decision.

Not much more time passed before Jack married his friend, and everyone seemed to finally settle down. We bought the house from Jack, and the kids were able to stay put for awhile.

I worked full-time, close to the children's school, and Wally worked just a few blocks in the other direction. Our neighborhood area had everything we needed, but we would venture downtown for the Fourth of July and Christmas parades and an occasional Bucks game, and many Tuesday nights, we'd go to a doubleheader Brewers game with the children. At one of our Brewer adventures, there was a game delay due to rain. During that delay, John and a friend went through the stadium collecting plastic beer cups, making a chain of those cups to cover several sections. The Milwaukee Journal newspaper took a picture of that event and it ended up on the front page.

Wally took John to an Admirals hockey game, and they got a hockey stick autographed by the players. John has that hockey stick to this day.

Wally became very involved with Julie's softball team and coached them for a couple of years. He also coached John's basketball team. I helped the cheerleading coach for Julie's cheerleading squad.

One day, when I went back to the office after lunch, there was a huge stack of papers on my desk with a note that read, "Dear Suzanne, I was called out of town for an indefinite period of time and I trust you will be happy to take over the coaching of the cheerleaders." "Just what I needed," I thought.

I reluctantly took over but found that it was such a rewarding activity for me that I stayed on for ten years. Julie was long gone from that school, and I was still organizing the squad, having annual tryouts for the cheer-leaders and enjoying every minute with the girls. By this time, one of the cheerleaders that had been there from the start of my career with them asked if she could take over.

Wally was doing very well at his job at Allied, and he enjoyed the work, too. However, when their pool installer came over to meet with him one day, I heard them talking about opening up their own business selling spas and hot tubs. Soon, he gave his notice at Allied, and he and his partner opened up Spas Etcetera. To make me feel like a part of their business, they let me name their store. I initially opposed his leaving Allied because he was doing so well in the swimming pool business.

Spas Etcetera was open for over a year. They had a lot of traffic in the store, and every once in awhile, I would don a swim suit and enjoy a hot spa time at the store. There were always a lot of lookers at the store, but spas and hot tubs were very new to the area, and people were slow to purchase.

His former boss, Dick, would surface at Spas Etcetera from time to time and tell Wally that if he ever wanted to go back to Allied, he was welcome to do so. After about a year and a half with too many lookers and not enough buyers, Wally decided it was time to go back to Allied. Fortunately, he was welcomed back as if he had never left.

In the year and a half that Wally was in the spa business, he had to take a night guard job downtown at a warehouse. It was tough on him, and he got very little sleep and even less pay. Life proved to be very good the second time around at Allied. This was a happy time for us.

PART III

CHAPTER 15

HE CALMED
TROUBLED WATERS

THE year was 1979. Though I was content in my life
with Wally and the children, I felt something was
missing. Remember all of those rosaries I said? I thought I
knew the Lord. I don't recall anyone ever telling me that we
are saved by the blood of the Lamb, Jesus Christ. I knew
I needed to learn more about Him, and I had a yearning
to know the contents of the Holy Bible. We were never
encouraged to study the bible in the Catholic Church at
that time. Thank God, things have changed.

My boss was on the committee to set up and welcome
Billy Graham to Milwaukee County Stadium in August,
1979. I was invited to work with this committee, but
due to an upcoming surgery, I had to decline. That Billy
Graham was coming to our town intrigued me.

Wally, John, and I decided to attend the three-day
event. My brother, Billy, had just broken up with his girlfriend, and when he called to come for a weekend visit, we
invited him to join us at this Christian gathering.

After the service on Friday night, there was what they

called an altar call. An altar call is where everyone who
has any reason whatsoever to ask God's forgiveness and
accept Christ as their personal savior is welcome to come
forward. I get good goose bumps just thinking about this
time in my life.

I didn't look one way or the other to see if anyone was
going to join me. I knew where the car was, and I knew
they wouldn't leave without me. I stood up, and with tears
streaming down my face to the point that I could hardly
see, I went forward.

The choir sang, "Just as I am without one plea; but
that Thy blood was shed for me. And that Thou bidst me
come to Thee; Oh Lamb of God, I come, I come!"

Though it seemed to take forever to get to the center
of that field, I didn't care. I was spiritually healing with
every step. A gentleman approached me in the center of
that field. He was gathering groups of five or six people to
give those groups some information about Bible studies.

As I dried my eyes, I looked around, and even though
there were thousands of people going forth to give their
hearts to the Lord, I spotted Wally, John, and my brother,
Billy, coming toward me. We hugged each other. Everyone
was teary-eyed, especially my brother, Billy. He said he was
also feeling a healing from his broken relationship.

Nothing else seemed to matter. He Calmed Troubled
Waters right there on the spot. We had found the Lord
in a new way, and life was changing for each of us as we
stood and listened to our coach. He prayed with us and
encouraged each of us to seek out a Bible study. The Billy
Graham Organization followed up with a phone call to

our home within a few weeks after that event. We had already gotten involved in weekly Bible studies.

My brother went back to Menasha, and he, too, sought out Bible studies, eventually becoming an ordained minister for the Lord, leading people to Him on a daily basis.

This proved to me that even though I was so lost in my own self for so long, God never left me, not for one moment. My eyes were finally open. The days were brighter, no matter what the weather. I found I wasn't searching for happiness anymore. Happiness comes from within, and there isn't another living being, item of clothing, piece of jewelry, cocktail party, or master bridge points that will bring real happiness.

CHAPTER 16

BIBLE STUDIES
IN OUR HOME

AFTER attending the Billy Graham Crusade, Wally's Uncle Carl started coming to our home once a week to help us get started with our study of the Holy Bible. He was a godly man who knew his Bible inside out. One by one, our neighbors joined us, and it was a very special time of our week. John also took pride in our weekly studies.

We started attending a prayer group at our neighborhood church. One night, John said he'd better not go to prayer group because he had to study for a test. I suggested that he go and pray about his exam. He did. The next day he was happy to tell me that he got his first "A." He was really hooked on bible studies and prayer groups from then on. Actually, John and his wife are in Mexico on a missionary trip with their church as I type this.

Our prayer group leader approached me one evening and asked if I would like to teach religion classes to the grade school children. My prompt answer was, "Absolutely not; I cannot teach the children what was drilled into me." He said, "Then you really need to look into teaching so you can learn the changes that the Catholic Church is making." Upon further thought, I began looking into teaching lessons for young children. After perusing the lessons, I decided that the leader of our prayer group was right.

I began teaching the three-year-olds while their parents attended Sunday Mass. This was so rewarding to me. I then taught third graders about the Bible and Jesus.

One day, just before classes started in the fall, as I was closing my classroom door, I noticed a man walking down the corridor, holding the hands of two young boys. I asked him which classroom he was looking for.

His answer crushed my spirit! He said, "I missed the deadline, and we'll have to wait until next year." Without hesitation I asked what grades his boys were in. He said one was in second grade and the other was in fourth grade. I said, "Guess what. I'm teaching third grade, and they are both welcome to join my class." They did. Come to find out, the Dad was newly divorced and wanted his boys to learn about God.

The boys did very well in my class. They were happy kids, and I thoroughly enjoyed both of them. A few months after my class ended for the season, I received a note from the boys' father. He thanked me and invited me to the boys' baptism. I was thrilled to witness the baptism of these two young boys. God had chosen me to be instrumental in their lives.

JULIE AND BIBLE STUDIES

Julie, on the other hand, was very skeptical about

joining us. She would walk right through the living room during our Bible studies and go to her friend's house, or she would go to her bedroom and watch television. She wanted nothing to do with Bible studies at that time. After she walked out, I would be upset. Uncle Carl would calmly say. "Let's pray for Julie." He did, and with his thunderous voice, he would spiritually lift Julie up to the Lord. When he finished praying, he would look at us and say. "Let's be patient now, and wait upon the Lord." I have never met anyone like Uncle Carl Frank. I think the Lord heard Uncle Carl even when he whispered.

Julie attended the University of Stout at that time. One Sunday, just before her ride was going to pick her up at our home and take her back to school, Julie started crying uncontrollably. She cried and cried, and I sat by her on the couch, wondering what was wrong. She just sobbed and hugged me and said, "Mom, I want what you, John, and Wally have. I want to know the Lord." Since our time was short, I prayed with her, and I advised her to settle down and seek out a Bible study group on campus. She calmed down immediately, and it wasn't long before she was calling me with all sorts of happy news about her new life in the Lord.

One day, when Wally and I were in Minneapolis attending Julie's church service on Mother's Day, Julie got up to give her testimony. This surprised me, and we were all crying by the time she finished. She said right there in front of God and everyone, "Mom, I want you to know that while I was in my room, supposedly watching television when Uncle Carl was over, I had my ear up to the door, listening to everything that was said." Needless to say, that was a happy day and made a wonderful Mother's Day gift.

In 1977, we received a call that my Dad had died. He had been in the hospital over Christmas 1976. Though he was able to be with us for our Christmas Eve gathering, he had to return to the hospital shortly afterward for another week or so.

It was mid-February. A friend of Dad's asked him to go with him and pick water- cress in the stream. Dad was showing Elmer how to find and pick the cress when he fell down, face first into the water. His heart had given out. Dad was gone at the young age of sixty-three.

It was heart-warming to see so many of the grownup kids from the area at Dad's funeral. They all remembered Frank Waters from Frederick St., Menasha, Wisconsin, and all he had contributed to the community. He helped not only his own family of ten, but many other young-sters get interested in hobbies and sports. He will always be missed by many.

CHAPTER 17

LIFE IN THE EARLY EIGHTIES

IN 1980, Mom and I were planning a trip to Europe, and in order to get some extra cash, I had my first ever rummage sale in Milwaukee. I made $1,500, which was enough to cover my entire trip, including meals, flight, touring, and spending money.

We toured five countries in Europe with a church group from Neenah. The highlight of the trip was spending a day in Oberammergau for their passion play. Mom and I had tickets in the second row of that huge coliseum. It was a memorable and very enlightening time for both of us. Mom had been there in 1970, so she was familiar with the performance. Most of the people in Oberammergau take part in this passion play. It is performed every ten years, honoring God for sparing people's lives during the Black Plague.

Wally and I used to tent camp on our land in the woods of Waupaca. We'd go on Friday after work and would drive home early Monday morning in time to shower, get John to school, and go to our jobs.

One time, when we were driving home to Milwaukee, I said, "The closer we get to the big city, the more I feel like a violin whose strings are being tightened." I was truly becoming disenchanted with the pace of the city. It was buzz-buzz, hurry-hurry, with everyone rushing here and there.

I worked full-time in the city so we could make ends meet. I loved my job, but the company had acquired new owners, and things were changing rapidly.

I asked Wally if there was any chance that we could build a house on our property in the woods in Waupaca. Before he went back to work with Allied, he had suggested several times that we move to Waupaca and live a simple life.

A couple of weeks later, Wally called me from work and said, "About that little house in the woods in Waupaca … " He was ready to talk about it. One thing led to another, and before we knew it, we were paving the way for a possible move. We took a day off work and drove to Waupaca to talk to Mr. Myers at the Waupaca Area Chamber of Commerce. He said that with our skills, there would be plenty of opportunity for us to get jobs.

John got wind of our possible move and said he wouldn't mind, but he'd like it if we could move before he started his senior year. He was a junior at Dominican High School in Whitefish Bay at the time. Julie was a freshman at Stout. We decided to call her and see what she thought about our possible move. She said she had made friends from all over, and she didn't care one bit if we decided to move to Waupaca.

We had a plan. I went to my boss first with the news

that I might be moving up north. As usual, he was a gentleman and wished me well, but he made me promise to give six weeks' notice since I was so familiar with the company and he was away a lot.

It didn't take long for word to get around in Waupaca that an executive secretary and a retail salesman were moving to town. I received a letter from Fran at a bank in Waupaca asking if I cared to come in for an interview. I asked my boss for some advice. He said I shouldn't close any doors. He encouraged me to write to Fran and explain that a lot of things had to take place before we made our move. I did.

Next, Wally went to the owner of his company. His boss said he was thinking about having Wally move up to his Appleton store, but he wasn't sure when to do this. This was great news for us because Appleton is just thirty-five minutes from Waupaca. We were getting excited about our new venture.

We had a realtor put our Milwaukee home on the market. The family who purchased our home needed a couple of months before the closing could take place. That was fine with us because I had to give a six week notice at work.

Meanwhile, I saw an ad in the Milwaukee Journal looking for a person in Central Wisconsin to represent a Philadelphia Wicker Company. I met with a representative from that company and ended up starting my own business in early 1981.

Before leaving the area, I made an appointment with my doctor for an annual checkup. When I told him we were moving up north, he suggested that I try living there before just moving there. He said, living in the woods in a small town area would be a whole new lifestyle. He cautioned me again and again that day, but I chose to ignore his prompts, and we moved ahead with our plans.

The next couple of months were spent packing and getting ready for our move, planning with Waupaca builders for our new home, and other such things.

We had an appointment to meet our buyers at the bank in Milwaukee at 3:00 PM on moving day. The time was getting close. The loaded truck had left the neighborhood with all of our belongings. The phone rang at 1:00 PM. Our buyer, Mike, said, "Sorry but my loan fell through." Oh my! Now what? I had an idea instantly. I asked him if he had twenty thousand dollars to put down. He said that he did. We agreed to meet at the bank, and I called to have the papers changed to a land contract. We all signed the papers, and by 5:00 PM, we were headed north.

We stayed at my family homestead on Frederick Street in Menasha while our home was being built in the woods of Waupaca. It was fun to be back there for awhile after twenty-one years of living in the big city.

My sister Kathy and her husband, Ted, were leaving for a vacation, and I was in charge of caring for their three-year-old daughter, Beni. I was so relaxed in my new life. The pressure was gone. I wasn't accountable to anyone. Life was fun.

I took Beni to the same park that I had played in years earlier. She loved the swings as much as I did. One day, when we were at the park, Beni asked to go back home.

She was newly potty trained, and I needed to act fast. We walked back and forth to and from the park three times, but it seemed the urge would stop when we arrived at the house. Finally, on the third try, I set up a little table in front of the potty for her. I gave her some crayons and a coloring book, thinking that if she relaxed a little, we would get results.

I knew that Mom would have some aids for children in her cabinets, so I started searching. I broke off the tiniest corner from a piece of Ex-Lax and gave it to Beni. Results followed almost immediately, and little Beni had a big smile when she said, "Sanks for the schocolate, Aunt Sue."

John started school in Waupaca in September 1981. He stayed with Mom at her cottage while we remained in Menasha for awhile. Construction of our home was scheduled to be complete in October. John went to basketball games, got involved in the band, and made a lot of friends at Waupaca High School.

We moved into our new home on October 19, 1981. We had an early snowstorm that winter, and I thought I had died and gone to heaven. It was so gorgeous; the white snow on the green pines, an occasional red cardinal, and the gorgeous blue jays made a picturesque scene. According to Wally and me, we lived in the most peaceful setting in the world. There was very little traffic in our area, so the snow remained white most of the winter. I would cross country ski from right outside my door for miles. It was a welcome change from life in the big city.

We weren't even in our home for a year when I wrote to my doctor in Milwaukee, telling him that I should have moved from Milwaukee a long time ago. I loved the tranquility and the peace and quiet that country living afforded us.

I wanted to join the Catholic Church, but I was concerned because I had not had an annulment before marrying Wally. I asked God to guide me. Again, I felt that people may turn me away, but I knew that God would not. Wally and I made an appointment with the priest. He listened to our entire story. We were overjoyed when he stood up, shook our hands, and said, "Welcome to the church." He explained that the annulment of a marriage was designed to help people clear their consciences and move on with their Christian walks. He felt that we had already done that. God bless him for thinking outside of the box. That priest was a true Christian.

It didn't take Wally and me long to get involved in the church. I again agreed to teach the children. We took over the coffee and donut program, coordinating the Sunday schedule and filling in when we were needed. We did this for ten years.

Mom and I also started a senior social afternoon at the church. People really enjoyed getting together, playing cards, and socializing. People made friends with others, and we enjoyed being a part of that.

One day I asked John why he was so much more outgoing in the small town school verses the big city school. He admitted that one by one, he saw his friends turn to drugs, and he wanted no part of it, so he opted to stay home.

When our Waupaca neighbor said he was going to

butcher some chickens, I offered John's help. I thought it would be a good experience for him. Reluctantly, John donned an old jacket and proceeded to help our neighbor. When he was finished, he came home and said, with a grudge in his voice, "Thanks a lot, Mom." Of course, it's fun to hear him tell the story to his children now; about the chickens running wild sans their heads.

It was after he worked at a tree farm, shearing Christmas trees for two summers, that John decided to go to college. One day, he came home from work, sunburned, with plenty of mosquito bites and one eye swollen shut from a bee sting. He threw his cap high in the air and said, "I'm not going to work this hard for the rest of my life, I'm going to college." I knew he meant it. I encouraged him to buckle down, study hard, and form good study habits, and he did. He was accepted at Stout University in the fall of 1983.

Wally and I got used to the empty nest very quickly. He worked all day, and I kept busy with my wicker business. I was the top sales person several months in a row. Initially, I sold wicker baskets and furniture at in-home parties. I loved getting my orders and would spend hours going through the exotic wicker items, packing the individual orders and making deliveries. Eventually, I sold to retail outlets in our state. The business was a nice weaning from the big job in Milwaukee.

While out on business one day, I experienced a very scary event, and it gives me goose bumps to recall it.

There had been several unsolved murders in the Madison area around the time, and I was well aware of that as I headed out. I had finished my business for the day, having visited my accounts between Waupaca and Madison, and was headed back home.

I decided to stop for something to eat. As I was finishing my meal, while looking over my day's sales sheets, I had a feeling that a man was watching me. I proceeded to pay my bill and stayed fully aware as I headed across the street to my car. It was probably quite obvious with all of the wicker pieces I had in my station wagon that I was a salesperson doing business in that area. The man followed me out of the restaurant.

Noticing that he had his car parked on the other side of the street, I thought I was safe. I pulled out of my parking spot and checked my rear view mirror. Oh, my goodness! He was making a u-turn right in the middle of downtown. My heart began to pound! This confirmed my premonition. I was being followed.

I pulled into a gas station and filled up with gas, thinking I could get away from him. He also stopped for gas.

I left the gas station, and it wasn't long before I was on the highway, in the country, in the middle of nowhere. I tried to speed up, but he caught up with me. I slowed down so he could pass, but he slowed down, too.

I saw a vegetable stand ahead on my left and opted to turn without using my signal lights. That didn't work, either, and he followed me in. I quickly told the man and lady tending the stand that I was being followed by the man who was getting out of his car. They said they would try to keep him back. I picked out a couple of things, paid, and left. He bought nothing, got into his car and started to follow me again. I didn't have a car phone. I was so scared! Once again, I was praying my heart out. I reached over for my garage door opener and I put it to my mouth like I was talking into a phone while I looked into my rear-view mirror, pretending to get his license plate number.

What happened next happened so fast I could barely think. There were truly angels in my midst. Two Doberman Pinschers came running from across a field to my right. I was able to avoid them and was so taken aback by this that I almost forgot about the man following me. When I looked in my rear view mirror, he was gone, and there were no dogs in sight. I breathed a sigh of relief. I never saw his car again.

I stopped at one of my accounts in the next town. I walked in the door and immediately started shaking and crying. The proprietor said, "Suzanne, what's wrong?" After I related the story to her, she wanted to call the police immediately. I wanted to get the heck out of town! She gave me a bottle of water, and we chatted for a minute until I calmed down.

When I arrived home and relived the incident to Wally and John, they made light of it and asked, "What's for supper?" It was good to be back with my family. I wanted to forget this incident, but it stayed with me for a long time.

Although Mom loved to travel, she had never been to a tropical island. Through my business, I won a trip for two to St. Thomas, Virgin Islands. It was Wally's busiest time at work, and he couldn't get time off, so I invited Mom to join me.

Mom and I had a great vacation, but something happened the last night of our trip that could not only have ruined our trip, but it could have ruined our lives. Thank God for Mom's common sense.

Mom and I sat at the pool most of the afternoon. This was in 1982, and in those years we both loved the sun. I had gotten a little sunburn, so when it came time to go down for happy hour, I dressed in a light sundress with a swim suit underneath, and since I didn't want to wear any makeup, I wore dark glasses and donned a straw hat. I was young and probably looked a little flirty, but I was with my Mom, so I knew I was safe.

We each had a couple of glasses of wine. The band was playing, and suddenly I heard them say, "This song is for Suzanne." I popped off of my chair and proceeded to dance around the floor, feeling dizzy and a little disoriented, but, all in all, I felt okay. Everyone was clapping and singing, and we had a great time.

Then, I noticed that Mom started to walk away. I thought, "Oh, she is probably tired and just wants to go to bed early," so I proceeded to talk to other friends I had met through the wicker company. A few minutes later, another mother and daughter twosome came up to me and said, "Suzanne, your mother is standing around the corner by the door and she wants you to go up to the room with her **now**." Though I really didn't want to leave, I didn't want to upset my Mom.

I started walking toward the door when a man approached me, took my arm, and said, "Come on, I have a taxi waiting." I struggled, and I was able to pull away from him. With that, my Mom yelled at the man saying, "That's my daughter, and she's coming with me." I really knew she meant business and I humbly sauntered her way.

I had never heard my Mom raise her voice like that, so I knew she was upset.

Once in our room, we didn't say a word. I begrudgingly lay down on the bed, upset. I had my sunglasses on, my hat was on my head, and my dress and sandals were intact. I woke up in the same position with the sunrise in my face. It was then that I knew that somebody had spiked my drink.

I could relate to nasty things happening to innocent people while on vacation. Ignorance is not bliss in this case.

In 1982, a church group from the area invited Mom and me to attend a Charismatic Prayer Conference at Notre Dame over Memorial Day weekend. It was an awesome event. There were thousands of people gathered with one goal in mind: to praise the Lord. The teachings and singing inspired us. Among other things, we witnessed a man who had been confined to his wheelchair for ten years, get up and dance with his wife. His wife attested to the fact that it was a miracle of healing. There wasn't a dry eye among us.

On the way back home, we were talking about where we could go to join a prayer group. I had an idea that perhaps Mom and I could coordinate one right at our own church. I went to the front of the bus, took the microphone, and made the announcement. "Anyone in need of a prayer group or Bible study need look no further. Mom and I are going to get the ball rolling as soon as next week." We did.

Like Marion, many others who joined our class didn't know where to begin in the Bible. That Bible class is still

going on at the church, and its leader is—you guessed it—
Marion. "Ask and it will be given to you; Seek and you will
find; Knock and the door will be opened to you" (Matt.
7:7).

When I did in-home wicker shows, I started my
presentation with a brief personal testimony. When it
came time to pack individual orders, I inserted a small
Christian message in each package. I wanted to tell others
how God had helped me get through some difficult times
and encourage them to call on God and invite Him into
their lives if they hadn't already done so.

Lynn had attended one of my wicker shows. When I
ran into her in the grocery store, she wanted to know if I
could help her get started in her Bible. I asked her if she
had time that day. She followed me home from the grocery
store. I made us a little lunch, and I got my Bible out.

Lynn was struggling in her church and was having a
hard time accepting everything she was told. She wanted
to start searching scripture herself. I told her I gained a
personal relationship with God through recent Bible
studies and searching scripture on my own to learn more.
Though I never regretted my Catholic upbringing, I, too,
had a hard time trusting that I would learn everything
from a Sunday morning sermon. We said a little prayer
that God would open our eyes as we opened His book.

Being rather new to the Bible myself, I just opened
it at random and my eyes focused on the following verse,
Psalm 146:3 from the Good News Bible: "Don't put your
trust in human leaders; no human being can save you."
Wow! It didn't get much clearer than that. That was our
lesson for the day and we were both in awe at how God

had revealed that passage to us, since we had just talked about that subject.

Nearly ten years later, I received a lovely letter from Lynn. The day we opened the Bible together had a huge impact on her. She, too, had fallen in love with God's word and Bible studies. She was knocking, seeking, and finding. God truly opened her eyes the way He opened mine when I started searching for His word in Holy Scripture.

Wally and I bought two properties bordering ours in the woods. We had a campfire pit on each property and really enjoyed the peace and quiet. He left for work at eleven o'clock in the morning and didn't get home until ten o'clock in the evening. In the summer months, he'd drive up our driveway after a long day at work, and I'd have a campfire going. We would have a late supper, under the stars, while we listened to the whippoorwills, sometimes catching a glimpse of a raccoon or a deer.

My neighbor, Mary, told me to listen for the whippoorwills in early May. I asked what they sounded like. She made the bird's sound, and when I heard my first one, I was sure it was Mary outside of my house. I said, "Okay, Mary, you can come out now." When she didn't surface and the sound continued, I called her house. She answered. I was thrilled to hear my first whippoorwill.

Mother's cottage was through the woods from our house. She loved her cozy place, and Wally and I enjoyed having Mom all to ourselves. I never got much of a chance to visit with Mom when I lived in Milwaukee, and I would go to Menasha for weekend visits. She was always so busy, working full-time and spending most of her weekends in the kitchen, preparing food for the family. It was a hug "hello" when we arrived and a hug "goodbye" when we left.

I kept pretty busy, myself, with my business and other projects, but I always made time for Mom. She was pretty independent and loved her quiet time after all those years tending to her large family. She always had banana bread and coffee ready for me, no matter what time of the day I popped in.

Mom and Dad started to build that cottage with hopes of spending lots of time there together once Mom retired. Though Dad's dream did not come true, Mom enjoyed the fruits of his labor.

Mom worked full-time for a couple more years after Dad passed away. Though the cottage was not complete, she decided to go ahead and have it finished. Along with the carpenters, each of us kids took turns helping Mom with the finishing touches. When she decided to move into the cottage permanently, she updated it to accommodate her year-round needs. When the time was right, she sold the Frederick Street homestead. Her new home in the woods was always called, "The Cottage."

Mom cleared a large path on her nearly four acres of land. I saw her walking her path daily. She placed wooden stakes by the tiny pine trees, and on each stake was the name of one of her many grandchildren.

It was heartwarming to see Mom enjoy her later years, mostly being content with herself, with frequent visits from her many children and relatives. Our youngest brother, Billy, had a home in Plainfield with his wife and four children. Mom loved to drive over there to visit them, and they enjoyed her company as well.

Wally and Mom hit it off well, and over the years that we were neighbors, Wally played Scrabble with Mom at least a couple of times a week.

Mom had a standing invitation to join Wally and me on Saturday nights. In the summer, we had chicken cook-outs on the tripod over the campfire. Sure enough, around six o' clock in the evening, we would see Mom walking through the woods towards our house with her Manhattan in one hand and a dish to pass in the other.

In the winter, we often dined at our house or went out to dinner with Mom on Saturday nights. After dinner, we would challenge Mom to a game of cards, and she always took us to the cleaners.

I don't remember Mom and Dad ever having a cock-tail before dinner when we were kids. That would have been considered a luxury, and with ten kids to clothe and feed, they did without the extras. Once in a blue moon, they would go to the movie house, and they would talk about that movie all week.

As time went on, they both enjoyed golfing. Dad's friend, Joe Nadolny, was a golf pro, and occasionally he would give Dad and me a lesson. After Mom retired, she enjoyed golfing in a league until she was in her late eighties. Dad wanted all of us to at least try the sport. He loved nature and basked in the delight of seeing different species of birds and an occasional deer on the golf course.

Occasionally, I would enjoy my one-on-one chats with Mom over a glass of wine. It was one of these times that I said to Mom, "Didn't you ever just want to throw in your towel at some point when you were in the middle of raising so many kids?" She said, "Oh, sure, sometimes I wanted to jump off of a bridge, but I didn't have the time." Then she laughed and said, "Anyway, your Dad would have killed me."

CHAPTER 18

1984 AND BEYOND

AT the annual Allied Pool Christmas Party in Milwaukee, Dick, Wally's boss, announced that our 1984 Christmas party was going to be at a Chinese restaurant. There were several nice Chinese restaurants in Milwaukee, and we all wondered which one it would be. Surprise! Dick wanted all of us to celebrate the company's twenty-fifth anniversary in Taiwan and Hong Kong.

MOM'S HEART ATTACK

In December 1984, we got a call that our Mom had suffered a serious heart attack and was in the hospital in the area of Wally's workplace. The hospital was an hour away from our house but Wally was at work and agreed to go over and check on Mom. I knew many of my siblings would be with her, and I would wait my turn to visit.

We were planning to leave with twenty other people for our trip to Asia in a few days, and I wanted to make sure my Mom was okay before we left. I went up to the hospital and stayed overnight with some of my siblings as we waited for more news about our Mom.

I had a decision to make. I certainly wasn't in the mood to pack for our trip. How could I even think about going so far away at a time like this? I went in to peek in at Mom, and she said to one of the nurses. "This is my daughter who is going to the Orient in a couple of days." I thought, "Or not."

The doctors decided that Mom needed to have open heart surgery on December 31, 1984. I asked Wally if he would go on the trip without me. Luckily, he said no. That made up my mind. I didn't want him to miss out on an opportunity of a lifetime.

Mom loved to travel and was excited about this trip for Wally and me. We decided to take the risk and packed our belongings in a big hurry. We met the group for an overnight stay in Chicago before heading to the Orient the morning of January 1, 1985.

New Years' Day brought a huge snowstorm to Chicago. We had to fly to Minneapolis to pick up the flight crew that was stranded there.

Patti tried to page me at the Minneapolis Airport moments after we took off; Mom had taken a turn for the worse immediately following the surgery.

Due to all of the snow delays, we missed our connection in Tokyo and had to stay in a hotel there until the following morning. None of us had any extra clothing or essentials, and our luggage was way ahead of us. We dined in a fancy Tokyo restaurant that night, but the only thing on my mind was my Mom. I couldn't even think of eating.

Another reason why I couldn't eat was because nobody could identify any of the food. The wait staff was impressive in their native dress, but they couldn't communicate with us.

One thing I could identify was the bottle of Coke. Coca-Cola was written in Japanese on the bottle. I saved that empty glass bottle, packing it carefully and bringing it all the way back to Wisconsin. I let an organization borrow it for a display and haven't seen it since. Perhaps that is one of the reasons why I never get too attached to material things.

As soon as we landed in Taiwan, I telephoned Patti to see how Mom was doing. All was going well at that point, and Mom was resting comfortably. She seemed to be over the critical stage.

TAIWAN

Dick had been going to the Orient for twenty-five years, buying for his store for Christmas time, so he was familiar with the finest restaurants in both Taiwan and Hong Kong

The Oriental people have their cameras going constantly. We would go out in the middle of the night, and it looked like mid-day. Everything was lit up, and there were people everywhere. Everybody was clicking away with a camera.

Though Christmas is a Christian holiday, there wasn't one building in Taiwan that didn't have its entire edging outlined with tiny white Christmas lights. If you have witnessed the lights in Las Vegas, take that times one hundred, and you begin to fathom the streets of Taiwan at night. It was an awesome sight.

Ivory and brass were so prevalent that I couldn't even think of purchasing it. Everywhere we looked, in every store, we saw hundreds and thousands of pieces of ivory and brass. It subtracted its value, in my eyes. I guess that's the way it is with most things: supply and demand. The supply was in Taiwan, and the demand for the supply was in the United States, and by the time the supply gets to the United States, the price jumps sky high. There are great lessons to be learned through travels, for sure.

While in Taiwan, we lodged at the President's Hotel. Everywhere we went, we witnessed people sitting on the curb, slurping egg drop soup. The whole town and everything we owned smelled like sushi and the oriental food. Weeks after we got back home, I could still smell Taiwan.

We went to a place that had brand-name knockoffs. I bought a Rolex watch for $30.00. It looked expensive, and it is a fun keepsake. I needed a battery for it, and a jeweler took one look at my Rolex, threw his hands up in the air, and said, "Wow! I'm not touching that!" I had to chuckle as I walked away. I'm sure he took it for a real Rolex. In my eyes, the value of my pseudo Rolex had just went up!

HONG KONG

Up until this visit, I had been unaware of the vast differences between Taiwan and Hong Kong. Back in the mid-eighties, Hong Kong was known as the Trade Center of the World. I finally grasped this at the Hong Kong airport. Our group was escorted to the Regent Hotel in nothing less than a Rolls Royce. There were five of them lined up for our group.

Since Dick was known by many of the towns' people, we received top-notch care throughout our stay. Each night, we would be escorted to a different restaurant for dinner on the company's dime. There would be three round tables set up for us. At each table, a person from the area who spoke English would entertain us, answering questions and familiarizing us with the different foods.

Much to my regret now, Wally and I opted to stay back the day the group took a tour of a Buddhist Temple. In hindsight, we should have gone because it was going to be a once-in-a-lifetime experience. I was so into my Christian walk that I would not allow myself to even visit another religious site. You live and you learn.

We were hardly at our hotel for five minutes that first night when Dick made the announcement that we all had to meet back in the lobby in thirty minutes because we were headed on a sunset cruise of the China Sea to Jumbo's Floating Restaurant. I was so exhausted by this time that I wanted to skip this event. The mental strain of keeping in touch with the home front regarding Mom's health and all of the past week's activities had caught up with me. Wally and I made a pact to stick together, so upon second thought, I decided that this was his trip, and I should participate. Good thing that I did.

It was an awesome sight, being on the China Sea at sunset. The moon was rising at one end of the sea, and the sun was setting at the other. I didn't know where to look and decided not to have my eyes behind the camera. I just enjoyed the gorgeous setting. Going past all of the shrimp boats with their day's catch of plenty, along with their clothes drying on the line in plain view, was a sight to behold. Entire families spend months on these shrimp boats. That scene is etched into my mind.

Soon, we came upon Jumbo's Floating Restaurant. It was a huge building made into a boat for dining in the middle of the China Sea. We had the best meal, and I had the time of my life. It was one of those experiences that you had to be there in order to appreciate. I was glad that I let my optimism take over and hide my tired feelings that night.

Cabbage Patch Dolls were the rage in the United States at that time. I was happy to purchase Melinda in Hong Kong, where the dolls originated. I paid thirty U.S. dollars for her, and that was not much less than what they were selling for back in the States. Though it was not a deal, monetarily, it was a story. Somewhere along the line, Julie claimed the doll, and I haven't seen Melinda since.

Our visit to a kindergarten in China was so special. Those little children sang their hearts out for the tourists, and I could hardly see through the camera lens because of blurry vision from teary eyes. The children were so happy to have us pick them up and to have their pictures taken with us. It was an event that I will never forget.

We took a hydrofoil—a boat that is propelled to fly inches above the water—to Macaw, Red China. It was a tense time for us because we were told ahead of time that if any one of the group got sick over there, we would all have to stay until the person recovered. That put us on edge and we were all happy to get through that day. There were uniformed soldiers everywhere.

We toured China by bus. The area was in the process of building its very first golf course, which we passed en route. I also learned that the people in China were only allowed to have one child. Coming from a large family, I could not relate to that.

At one point, we visited a village in China. I remember a home that had a television set. They had it covered with a table cloth; televisions were very rare in China and considered a luxury. If you had one, and you didn't have it turned on, you kept it covered.

When the time came to leave the Orient, most of us were ready to go home. Although we all took great precautions regarding food and drink on our way overseas in order to avoid jet lag, we had a big party that last night and didn't watch what we consumed. It made a huge difference as far as jet lag was concerned.

I was grateful that I was not working at that time because not only did I come home with a nasty cold, but I couldn't get motivated for several days. I would wake up each day, take care of needs, trip over unpacked suitcases, and go back to bed. Sometimes, I would still be asleep when Wally got home from work. He assured me that I was not the only one. Several of the group were exhausted. All in all, it was a very memorable trip, and we were glad we had made the decision to go despite Mom's grave health situation.

Mom still had her home in Menasha, and my daughter, Julie, was on holiday break from Stout Univeristy. Julie stayed with her grandmother for awhile, during Mom's post-heart surgery days.

As soon as my cold was gone, I headed over to spend

some time with Mom. It was hard to see our Mom go through the natural post-operative depression. In all of the years that we had known our Mom, we had never, ever seen her down and out. A few years later, while working in the mental health field, I learned that depression is a very common occurrence following open heart surgery.

Even though it seemed to take longer than we expected, our Mom regained her strength and became her old self again. She came back to Waupaca and got back into her daily walking routine. Wally and I were glad to be close enough to give her a little extra help with her household chores, but she insisted on doing most things by herself. She was back on the golf course with her league the following spring.

It wasn't long until Mom moved to Waupaca full-time. I wanted to help her get involved in the community, and I knew she liked bowling, so I formed a team, and we joined a Monday afternoon league.

CHAPTER 19

BRIDGE GIRLFRIENDS AND THEIR RECIPES— END OF THE EIGHTIES

THOUGH our Monday bridge group started back in 1982, it took awhile to really get organized. We started out with three tables and one teacher. I was in a couples' bridge group in Milwaukee, but after quite a hiatus, I needed lots of lessons.

Our teacher, Sharon, was very patient with our group. We met every Monday at Linda Y's house because she had committed to caring for a friend's baby. Baby Joe slept all morning, probably because he couldn't get a cry in edgewise.

There was mass confusion at first. Somebody was always missing, and we would move a dummy from table to table to help with the bidding.

Little by little, people started leaving the bridge table for jobs and other pursuits, and I had the idea to get down to one table of serious bridge players.

As of this writing, Linda, Margaret, Mary Ellen, Karen, and I meet every Monday morning for twenty-four hands of bridge. Linda and Margaret trade off so there are always four of us to play competitively. It is a wonderful way to keep the brain sharp because our minds are never at rest during a bridge game.

This group also initiated duplicate bridge in our town, and Jack Rhodes is our director.

KAREN'S HEAVENLY ONIONS

This is a bridge luncheon favorite.
Make the day before and refrigerate.
2 large white sweet onions—slice in to rings
½ lb. fresh mushrooms
½ lb. shredded Swiss cheese
10 (or more) slices of French bread, buttered
1 can cream of chicken soup
½ cup of milk
2 tsp. soy sauce
Pepper to taste
1. Sauté onions and mushrooms
2. In a 9" × 13" baking dish, layer onions & mushrooms, Swiss cheese, and bread slices
3. Pour soup mixture over all
4. Bake uncovered at 350 degrees for 30 minutes

Mary Ellen's
Egg and Sausage Casserole

¾ lb. ground pork, browned and drained

6 bread crusts

Butter both sides of bread and cut into cubes

½ cup shredded cheese

6 eggs, beat with mixer

2 cups half-and-half

1 tsp. salt

1 tsp. dry mustard

1. In a 9" × 13" baking dish, layer bread, sausage, and cheese.
2. In a separate bowl, combine eggs, half-and-half, salt, and mustard. Pour egg mixture over the layering. Chill overnight, and remove from refrigerator 1 hour before baking.
3. Cover with foil and bake at 350 degrees for 40–50 minutes
4. Note: Top with chopped tomatoes, parsley, or whatever sounds good. Use your imagination!
5. Enjoy!

Margaret's Enchilada Soup

Makes A Lot

3 lbs. chicken breast
16 cups water
1 cup margarine or butter
1 onion, chopped
2 cloves garlic, minced
3 stalks celery, diced
¼ tsp. cumin
15 oz. can diced tomatoes
8 oz. can diced carrots
8 oz. can diced green chilis
2 pts. sour cream
1½ cups flour
2 tsp. paprika
2 tsp. salt
Grated cheese
Green onion
Tortilla Chips

1. Cook chicken breast in 16 cups Water. Save all of the broth.
2. Chop chicken and set aside.
3. Melt 1 cup margarine or butter in separate pan. Add onion, garlic, and celery. Cook until tender.
4. Gradually add flour, paprika, and salt.

Slowly add reserved broth.

Cook until thickened, stirring constantly.

Add cumin, tomatoes, carrots, chilies, and sour cream.

Add chicken.

Serve over crunched Tortilla chips in individual soup bowls.

Sprinkle with grated cheese and fresh chopped green onions.

Faye's Pickle Slivers

2 quarts of thin-sliced pickles (do not peel)

2 tbsp. Salt

1 sweet onion, sliced thin

½ tsp. celery salt

Cover with ice cubes - Let stand two hours

Drain

Boil together 1½ cups sugar & ½ cup Vinegar. Let cool.

Pour over pickles and refrigerate.

Enjoy!

SANDY'S PEACH COBBLER

½ stick butter

¾ cup milk

1 cup sugar

¾ cup flour

⅛ tsp. salt

½ tsp. baking powder

2 cup fresh peaches with juice, sliced

1. Melt ½-stick butter in deep baking dish
2. Mix ¾ cup milk, 1 cup Sugar, and ¾ cup flour in separate dish
3. Add ⅛ tsp. salt and ½ tsp. baking powder to mixture
4. Pour dough over melted butter
5. Add peaches on top of dough
6. Bake at 350 degrees until golden brown

Note: Any canned or fresh fruit can be substituted.

NANCY'S BLUEBERRY PIE

You can substitute strawberries or raspberries.

1 cup water

3 cups blueberries

1 cup sugar

3 tbsp. cornstarch

1 baked pie shell

1. In a saucepan, simmer 1 cup berries in ⅔ cup water
2. Combine 1 cup sugar and 3 tbsp. cornstarch with ⅓ cup water
3. Pour into berry mixture and boil for one minute (stir constantly)
4. Place two cups berries in baked pie shell
5. Pour cooled mixture over top of berries in pie shell
6. Enjoy!

Late 1980s

Julie had been away from home for a few years, living with some college girlfriends and enjoying the Minneapolis area. Wally and I went to spend a few days with the girls. They invited us to join them in their weekly Bible class. We had a wonderful time.

Though the drummer on the stage made an impression on Julie, I wanted to know who the handsome, blond-haired, blue-eyed guy who was handing out the programs was. She said, "Oh, that's just Len. Come on, I'll introduce you to him."

I called Julie every Sunday, and one day her roommate said, "She's over talking to Len." Yes! I was hoping that she would get together with him. He glowed, and I knew that he would make a wonderful mate for Julie. I was right.

I was excited when I heard of their plans to get married. She was my only daughter, and I was ready to get involved in her wedding. Well, as it turned out, she had made all the plans, and she assigned me to put the program together for the church service, which was going to take place in Minnesota. We had decided I would help her pick out her wedding dress, but I got a call one day, and she said she had found the perfect dress and wanted to know if she could buy it. Of course! I was getting used to the fact that when my kids were happy, I was happy. Their union trumped my sadness of not being able to be more involved in their wedding plans.

I knew their hearts were right with God, and that was all that mattered to me. I didn't care that they had participated in a nondenominational church in their area. I was so happy that their extra activities involved prayer groups and Bible studies.

Julie and Len Twetan were married in a Christian church in Minneapolis on September 17, 1988. It was a very hot day, but we had fun.

My brother Billy's son Seth, who was five years old, was their ring bearer. Little Seth was excited because he thought he was going to wear a bear suit. He cried when they started dressing him in a little black tuxedo. He said, "But Mom, where's my bear suit?"

Though I used to look forward to the day when I could sit down with my daughter and have a glass of wine, I was proud of the fact that she chose not to use alcohol, tobacco, or drugs. My children were always smart about their choices. I started to think that perhaps I did something right in their upbringing.

One October morning in 1987, I stayed home from my daily aerobics class and got a substitute for the bridge table because I wasn't feeling up to par. Wally made sure the phone was close to me in case I needed to call my Mom. He left for work and wouldn't be home until around ten o'clock in the evening.

At some point, I called Mom to tell her that I would not be able to go bowling with her because I was under the weather. She stopped over before she left and wrote the phone number of the bowling alley down, just in case I needed her.

Something was terribly wrong. I had very little strength, was white as a sheet, and was spitting blood. I picked up the phone, dialed the number of the bowling alley, and when Larry answered, I couldn't speak. I just moaned and tried to ask for Cathy Waters. He asked, "Is this Suzanne?" I could barely say yes. He gave the phone to my mother, and she faintly heard "Get the ambulance."

The ambulance arrived in minutes, but my veins had collapsed, and they couldn't start the IV. They rushed me to the hospital. I was close to death. Dr. Jerry later told me that if I had not gotten to the hospital when I did, I would have gone into shock. I suffered from a bleeding ulcer. Slowly but surely, I recovered and got back to normal. I thanked God for sparing my life.

This event took its toll on me, and I decided to take it easy for awhile. I sold most of my wicker samples and took some time off for myself. My stressful years had prompted this illness.

⸙

I had been unemployed for a little over a year. Though I was content, I still had the desire to return to the office. In 1988, on our drive home to Waupaca from Julie's wedding in Minnesota, I told Wally that I wanted to look for an office job. Soon, I was searching the newspaper for something that would suit me.

I noticed that our new hotel in town was almost complete, and they were looking for employees. I went right for the top job, administrative secretary. I had two interviews, and they told me that I was second runner-up, and they would keep me in mind.

I had an especially great interview with Dr. and Mrs. Fico at the Mental Health Clinic of Central Wisconsin

(MHCCW). I briefly shared the time in my life where I needed in-house treatment while going through divorce, etc. It was either going to make or break employment for me with them, but I didn't care. I wanted to emphasize how important I felt it was to seek treatment for one's mental health when needed.

In no time at all, I was job-sharing, typing progress notes for hours at a time at MHCCW. This was a highly confidential position, and I took pride in my responsibility. My job in Milwaukee had been highly confidential, too, and I proved that I was very trustworthy.

A few years later, due to a boating accident, I had to undergo chiropractic treatment. The chiropractic office offered me a job at my second visit. Thinking it would be a good chance for another learning experience, I joined them. I had on-the-job training, and it worked out pretty well for awhile. However, due to personality conflicts, I didn't stay longer than a year.

Wally had some things involving his work that kept me busy for awhile which included me as a nun in a hottub in a television commercial. The theme of that commercial was that being in a hot tub was a heavenly experience. Though it was more fun than it was work, the camera crew took over fifty clips with me sitting in that hot water, dressed up as a nun. Wally was there encouraging me with each new clip. They finally got it right. By the time I got out of the hot tub I felt like a prune.

Another time, Wally was looking for a couple of people to sit in a portable spa at the Fox River Mall in Appleton. It sounded like fun. Karen and I donned our modest swimming suits and sat in the hot, swirling water for a couple of hours. Wally took a few spa orders that day and we were happy to help him out.

Not much time passed, and MHCCW called me back. This was quite a pat on the back for me, and I rejoined their staff for a couple more years.

⁓✸✸✸⁓

Wally and I couldn't imagine leaving our cozy home in the woods. Though we started out with a simple ranch home, we added a large room, which we called our lodge, and a two-car garage to our property.

We had a deck just outside of our kitchen patio doors. In just a few steps, we were in our pool. Our deck extended back to the lodge which had seventeen windows and a spa. It was a wonderful setting, and we enjoyed many hours of leisure in our home in the woods. We had what we called our "ethnic shelf" in the lodge. In our travels, we would purchase something to put on that shelf, and while spending soothing time in our spa, we would look over the items on that shelf, recalling our trips.

Our land in the pines was zoned recreational, and little by little, people were bringing their trailer homes in from the big cities. We could envision a campground atmosphere in the future.

Mom made it clear to us that she was staying put and that she certainly would not object to us locating elsewhere in the area. That opened the doors and prompted us to broaden our scope, and we began checking out other properties.

CHAPTER 20

THE EARLY NINETIES

WE lived in the woods from 1981–1992. One day,
toward the end of the eighties, I saw a home on a
river for sale. I talked Wally into going to look at it with me.
We both loved the property, but it needed a lot of work,
and Wally didn't have the time to devote to renovations.

Wally had driven past a place that he loved every day
on his way to work. He had pointed it out to me on several
occasions. He called me from work one day and said there
was a "for sale" sign on that property. I made an appointment with the realtor, and that evening, we were on the
site.

I was chatting with the realtor when I noticed that
Wally was standing on a pier. What? This property was on
a lake? Well, not only did we fall in love with the house,
but the property was to die for. It was six miles out of town
and about six miles closer to his work in Appleton. Life
was good!

We put our property in the woods on the market in
the beginning of 1992, and by the first part of August, we
were moving into our new home on Bailey Lake. It was
a much bigger home, and we had fun buying some new

things and furnishing this very unique dwelling. We had lots of plans for our new digs.

Julie and Len came to help us move, and before they left that weekend, she handed me a mug that said "Grandma," and she gave Wally a mug that said "Grandpa." Yup! She was pregnant with our first grandchild!

Julie made me promise that I would be with her for the delivery of her first baby. My car was packed when the time came close to her scheduled delivery date. I got the call while at work in the Stevens Point office on a Wednesday night. Julie said, "Mom I'm going to have the baby tomorrow." I told her I would be on my way shortly. I left the office and drove in a drizzly, sleety slush all the way to Minneapolis. When I arrived in Julie's driveway at eleven o' clock that night, I laid on the horn and praised God for my safe trip.

Julie met me at the door, and things progressed nicely the next day. Samuel Walter Twetan was welcomed into the world just as his Uncle John came on the scene. What an honor for me and Wally, that Julie and Len chose "Walter" as Sam's middle name.

Any new grandparent knows what followed. We spent as much time as we could in Minneapolis with our new grandson. Life couldn't get much better for us.

⸻

I accepted a part-time position at an upscale ladies clothing store, The Feminine Touch (F.T.). It was a great place to work, and I enjoyed the customers so much. The proprietor, Mary Jo, couldn't have been nicer to her employees.

Soon, it came time to boil down to one job, so I left MHCCW. The time spent with my grandson Sam, working my part-time job, and being a good wife to Wally was enough for me.

While working at the Feminine Touch, I met a gal named Kerry. She was young enough to be my daughter, and I sort of took her under my wing. She was Mrs. Waupaca County, and I paved the way for her to ride in a convertible in the Fourth of July parade. She and I got along well.

Five years later, Mom said she got a call from Ethel Waters' daughter. Ethel and I are second cousins, and I remembered spending lots of time with Ethel and her siblings on their farm up north as a youngster. I asked Mom what the girl's name was. Mom said she didn't think I would know her. She said, "Her name is Kerry N." I said, "Mom, I work with Kerry N." What a small world! I knew Kerry for five years before I realized we were related.

John didn't date much in high school or college. After graduating from Stout, he experienced a job in a neighboring town. That didn't last long. His sister encouraged him to move to the big city. He lived with Julie and Len for awhile and went job hunting every day. He found a nice job and housing and he grew to love big-city livng. When he came back to Waupaca for a visit, he had a new car with a Minnesota license plate.

Lia worked in the same office as John. He was in sales and was in and out of the office. Lia was trying to make contact with John, but he seemed hard to pin down. One day, she left her business card on his desk with a note that said, "Call me." He did. She cooked dinner for him that night, and soon they were dating on a regular basis.

A short time after they got engaged in 1992, we were all chatting about wedding plans; which town, which church, etc. They said they would rather go to Jamaica and have a quiet Christian wedding ceremony on the beach. We gave our approval. They were happy, and when our children were happy, we were happy.

Their son, Andrew, was born prematurely in December 1994. Those first couple of weeks, he had to stay in the hospital, fighting for his life. That was a challenge for all of us.

Wally and I arrived at the hospital in Minneapolis within hours after Andrew's birth. When John saw us, he started to put his jacket on. I said, "Where are you going?" He said, "Mom, there's a little problem.They had to move Andrew to Children's Hospital." Away we went.

Oh my goodness! If you could have seen Andrew, with all those tubes hooked up to his precious little body, you would have hurt, too. I was crying within my heart. Prayers started immediately.

The doctor came into the room shortly after we arrived. He looked at John and said, "I hate to say this, but I don't want you to get your hopes up too high. We had a little guy like this who didn't make it last week." The color in John's face and the sparkle in his eyes drained immediately. I had to leave the room because I didn't want him to see me crying.

When we got back to Waupaca, I tried to call the

church and get Andrew on their prayer list. I couldn't talk, I was so choked up. I said I would call back.

Life was difficult during those days. However, with good care and by the grace of God, Andrew grew into a healthy young lad.

We loved our unique home on Bailey Lake and had lots of plans to enhance the property. Any chance Wally had, he was planting shrubs, contemplating other changes, or just sitting on his pier fishing. We were on top of the world. Everything was going so well.

Wally got a nice promotion and was chosen to be second-in-command of the company. He finally worked nine to five, five days a week. There would be no more weekends at work for him. We were thrilled. I remember standing outside of the realtor's office when we signed the final papers on our Bailey Lake home, and we hugged each other, shedding tears of joy. It seemed like things were finally falling into place for us. We enjoyed some traveling and couldn't have been happier.

CHAPTER 21

IF YOU WANT TO MAKE
GOD LAUGH, MAKE PLANS

M Y sister, Kathy, introduced me to the saying, "If you want to make God laugh, make plans." It's true; we can make all the plans we want, but God is still in control.

It was late in 1995 that Wally started showing signs of a health problem. He had trouble breathing, and his blood count was goofy. He had a few transfusions, after which he would feel fine for a short time. This went on for a few months.

One time, I insisted that he go in for a thorough checkup. He did. He was immediately hospitalized with pneumonia. Boy! We sure weren't prepared for this.

Soon, he seemed well and things settled down for a few months, but not for long. Doctor Bob ordered a bone marrow biopsy. A few days later, he was called into the doctor's office. We learned that he had bone marrow cancer.

We were devastated! We immediately sought out prayer partners and attended one of my brother Jim's Bible studies where people laid hands on Wally and prayed. We prayed that God's will be done and that Wally would make the right choices. We also prayed for his comfort through it all.

Though we felt peace amidst the turmoil, it was hard for us to accept that his life might be shortened.

Many people encouraged Wally to get on a list for a bone marrow donor, but he initially wouldn't have anything to do with that. He called me from work one day and said, "Let's get plane tickets to Sedona, Arizona. I want to put the house up for sale and move to Sedona, where I will golf the rest of my days away." He was serious. I called my friend, Pat Ryan, who had told us about Sedona, and he immediately sent us some information that included the name of a realtor there. We got plane tickets and were going to spend our twentieth anniversary in Arizona, searching for housing.

Wally's doctor got word of our intentions and immediately told us that Wally's only chance of survival was the bone marrow transplant. He said Wally would not see his fifty-fifth birthday on August 4, 1996, if he didn't do this. After his immediate family tested negative, Wally agreed to be put on a list for a donor transplant. We had to put our trip to Arizona on hold.

Len was on the committee for Promise Keepers, a Christian men's group in Minneapolis. They were about to have a weekend of prayer, song, and worship, and they invited Wally. I never thought he would be able to get through that weekend because he was getting quite fragile as he awaited a donor for his bone marrow transplant. Len saw to it that Wally had a wheelchair, and they parked close to the entrance in order to make it more convenient.

At one point that weekend, Julie turned on the radio, and we heard sixty thousand men singing "How Great Thou Art." Chills ran down my spine and tears spilled down our cheeks at the sound of so many men praising God in unison. Promise Keepers weekend was a great help to Wally, and he took everything in stride.

During the weeks that Wally had to await a donor, I had two hundred pins made and passed them around to our friends in town and beyond. The pins said, "Hey Wally, we're with you all the way!" It helped to lift his spirits as he started his journey to unknown happenings.

On Wally's fifty-fifth birthday, my daughter, Julie, and my sisters gave a huge surprise birthday and going away party for him. A female donor had been found in central Europe, and we were headed for Froedtert Hospital in Milwaukee the following day so he could be prepared for the bone marrow transplant. Though Wally was only given a thirty percent chance for survival, it was a chance that he opted to take.

He worked at Allied right up until we went in for his lengthy hospital stay. We took it one day at a time. I glanced over at him as he was driving to Froedtert Hospital and said "A penny for your thoughts." It was then that I noticed tears running down his face. He seemed so strong through everything so far, however, he admitted to being afraid of the unknown. As always, we quickly said a prayer and felt immediate comfort.

I took the advice of the staff at the hospital and went for walks in the brisk fall weather every morning and afternoon. I never hesitated to share what Wally and I were experiencing. I talked with strangers while sitting on a park bench or walking in the leaves. I found comfort in talking to anyone who would listen. I believed they were God's angels sent to me at that difficult time.

The tape that Wally purchased at the Promise Keepers Convention provided many soothing hours of music to our ears during his three-month stay at Froedtert Hospital. I was with him every day from 7:00 AM to 7:00 PM.

After staying with our friends, Bob and Rikki, for the first month, Wally made arrangements for me to reside at the Marriot Residence Inn which was closer to the hospital. The daily cost of the inn was not covered by my insurance and I will be forever grateful to people from St. Mary Magdalene's Catholic Church in Waupaca for helping me with that expense. I think it is noteworthy to mention that I kept close records of my lodging expenses. The donations from the parishioners came to within a dollar of my lodging costs. Talk about a blessing!

Though his bone marrow transplant was successful, he began to contract several different lung diseases. Soon, he contracted a brain virus that slowly took his mind.

During the three and a half months that Wally was in the hospital, many visitors arrived to keep our spirits alive. We had originally told friends and family that we would go through this mission by ourselves, contacting them if need be. When his health seemed to deteriorat beyond repair, I picked up the phone and called close friends and family. My sister, Kathy, spent long hours and several days with us. Next, my friend, Nancy, came to keep us company.

I still keep in touch with the chaplin of the hospital,

Rev. Steve Stearn. He visited Wally on a regular basis and always had comforting words for me.

Our twentieth wedding was on October 30, 1996. Even though we were in the hospital and Wally was suffering memory loss from the the brain virus, I was determined that we would celebrate our anniversary together. It was a gloomy, rainy afternoon when I went to the Residence Inn to change clothes that afternoon. I got all dolled-up, as Wally would say. I wore a nice dress and heels, nylons etc. I purchased a bottle of non alcholic wine, and two wine glasses. After ordering his favorite meal from the Milwaukee Restaurant Taxi, I told the staff at the hospital to hold his tray because it was our twentieth anniversary and I was ordering out. I lit a couple of candles in his room and the atmosphere was nice. A few of the nurses and doctors peeked in from time to time with well-wishes. All the while that was going on, Wally kept saying "What are we doing this for?" No matter how many times I told him it was our twentieth wedding anniversary it just did not register.

When the food was all in place, and after saying a prayer, I started to eat, thinking that he would join me. Wally pushed his stand with the food aside and asked for his tray. Oh boy! I poked my head out the door and called for his dinner tray. I'm quite sure that the nurses could hardly keep from laughing. It was sort of funny, but by that time I just wanted to head back to the inn and settle in for the evening. I went back, poured myself a glass of wine and called a few friends to share the story. They always said the right thing and I was grateful that they were there for me.

Mom surfaced at the hospital several times; one time putting me on a plane so I could visit my children and grandchildren in Minneapolis. She stayed with Wally during my five-day absence.

When I boarded the plane for Minneapolis I had made up my mind not to talk to anyone. I was going to be in my own little world of thoughts and ponder where life was going. I was hardly seated when Carol, the gal next to me said, "So, are you coming or going?" I promptly replied, "I don't know." She snickered and said, "Neither do I." It turned out that she had just learned of her husband's affair and was on her way to see her children. We talked nonstop and before we parted ways, I learned that she worked at Froedtert Hospital. She made arrangements to meet me in Wally's hospital room the following week, on my birthday, and treat me to dinner at a fine restaurant in Milwaukee. Through the years, we have spent many good times together. Carol Ryan will always have a special place in my heart.

This next event is truly a miracle. After more than three months, we were told that Wally would not make it through the night! My heart was heavy, but we were all preparing for his next life, one in which he would be pain free and with his Savior.

Mom and I were standing by Wally's bed. He had been in a comatose state for nearly forty-eight hours. All he would do was moan. It was so sad. It broke our hearts. We took his hands and, not knowing if he would be able to hear us, we told him we were going to say The Lord's Prayer for him. His moaning ceased immediately, and he said the entire prayer, struggling with his speech, but without missing a word, while Mom and I stood there in complete silence, tears of joy and sadness running down our faces.

That night, November 18, 1996, Julie and Mom stayed in the lounge. The staff placed a hospital bed next to Wally's bed for me. His moaning continued through the night. I finally laid his hand over his chest and turned over. The nurse woke me ten minutes later to say that Wally had died.

Though this is hard for me to relive, I want to tell you that when the days seemed almost impossible to get through after Wally's death, I thought of the way his life ended: his final words were The Lord's Prayer. He died at 2:10 AM on November 19, 1996. We knew where he was going. Thank God that He, Mom, and Julie were with me.

Wally's doctor had asked to be called as soon as Wally died, no matter what time it was. John arrived shortly after the doctor came into Wally's room at 3:00 AM. The doctor was also a member of Promise Keepers. We all held hands as the doctor sang "Amazing Grace." Wally lay there, finally peaceful.

God called Wally home, and I rejoiced in this, no matter how hard it was to let him go.

A nun told a cute story to our fifth grade class, and it is a nice message to remember at a time like this. "Every time little Tommy would open a door, he would say, 'Hello God, here's Tommy.' On Tommy's deathbed, God opened a door and said 'Hello Tommy, here's God.'" I pictured the good Lord welcoming Wally into the eternal kingdom.

CHAPTER 22

LIFE MUST GO ON

THOUGH what happened following Wally's death is really insignificant, it means a lot to me to tell you how important it is to keep your head above the water during sad times. I knew I was either going to sink or swim, and I decided, with God's help, to swim. One thing I had going for me in this adverse situation was my faith in God. I knew He would take care of me. He did.

Instead of telling you all about my ten years as a widow, I'm going to name some people who made my life a little easier: the Catholic Church parishioners; my siblings; Monday morning bridge girls Karen, Pat, Margaret, Linda, and Mary Ellen; and Thursday bridge girls Sandy, Joan, Mary Ann, Faye, Nancy, Judy, Bonnie, Cecile, and Shirlee.

My coworkers at Feminine Touch and its proprietor, Mary Jo, were so helpful. Friends who helped me with chores, phone chats, hugs, or just kind words were Morrie N., Jan B., Doctor Bob, Ardelle and Russ M., Donna S., Betty M., Bob S., Margaret H., Phil and Alice S., Chris and Peter N., Tom and Joan R., Don P., Tom Mc., Jim K., Jim T., and Bill B. Tom H. was very helpful with my car repairs. Carol R., my airplane angel, will never be forgotten.

My neighbors were always checking on me. My coworkers at MHCCW were wonderful, with special attention given by Inez T. and Dave R., who were by my side and on call if I needed them. Mary and Jim F., proprietors of MHCCW; my boss and friend from Images Design, Elaine N.; and Marcia and friends from Faith Community Church showed much concern.

Waupaca Area Chamber of Commerce employees and volunteers supported me. High school friends from out of state who called often and opened their homes to me were Mary Jo C. from Texas, Patty R., Tom G. and Pat R. from California. Danis, my tennis partner, and her husband, Don J. were very attentive. Tom and Taffie from Arizona sent well-wishes. My prayer partner, Sandy C. from Wisconsin Rapids, and I were in touch weekly.

A special thanks to my children Julie and John and their spouses and my loving grandchildren. I made many trips to their homes. The comfort and support from them warmed my aching heart.

Both Julie and Lia were expecting during the duration of Wally's hospital stay, with Lia giving birth to Jack the day after Wally's funeral and Julie birthing Catherine Suzanne the following Valentine's Day. My children have been my blessings throughout my life, but especially in my widowed years. Thanks kids.

Finally, Mom and I became closer than ever. She had been widowed for nineteen years. She knew what it was like. We would often go to church services late Saturday and have dinner together after. We would chat about anything and everything. Mom told me she was on call for me. I could call or go over there anytime, day or night. Several times, I wanted to seek her soothing advice when I became anxious in the middle of the night. However, I knew if I started doing that, there would be no end. I would simply pray myself back to sleep. That was always comforting to me.

Also, I had a denim hat that I called my "attitude lid." When things weren't going smoothly, I would don my lid, and that always made me smile. That hat is hanging in eye's view in our home so I am constantly reminded to keep a positive attitude.

I want to thank all of you, who were involved in my life, from the bottom of my heart. You will never know what a difference you made in my life at a time when I needed you most.

I think it's good for everyone to continually reach out and try to help those in need. We never know what a difference we may make in someone's troubled times.

I was prompted to sell my home on Bailey Lake because I was so sad during those first few months. I could picture Wally sitting on that pier, fishing every evening at sunset. I knew I would miss him no matter where I went, but I felt that new surroundings would be good for me.

I met with some of my coworkers from the MHCCW. Even though it is recommended not to make any moves or major decisions within a year after losing a spouse, they knew me and knew it was going to be okay. So be it!

Fortunately, my home sold rather quickly, and I purchased a condo on the Chain of Lakes.

My long-time friend, Nancy, came and helped me tear my place apart and plan for a rummage sale. We took half of the things from my Bailey Lake home and put them in my garage, and I had a three-week sale. The home sat on a highway, so I would close the garage door at night and take down my sign. In the morning, I would put up the sign again and open my store.

It was fun on one hand, and on the other, it was sad to see all of Wally's fishing gear, his tools, and his personal items disappear. I got many hugs during this time from people who knew I was newly widowed. Several people came to help me, some of whom I didn't even know.

A complete stranger and his wife came back at the end of my sale. They helped me move large pieces of furniture to my new home and would not accept any money. They gave me a hug after a full day of moving things and were on their way. I haven't seen them since.

Several girlfriends pitched in and took carload upon carload from Bailey Lake to my Wingspan condominium on Waupaca's Chain of Lakes. It was fun to set up new housekeeping in my new location.

It is during these times that people truly make a difference in one's life. I believe there are angels in our midst.

This is a funny story: My good friend Karen held her tongue until I got settled in my new condo. Then, one day, we were sitting on my porch swing chatting, and she reminded me of something. She said, "Suzanne, I can remember a time when you, Wally, and I were on your porch at Bailey Lake talking about the what-ifs. Wally said, 'Oh, Suzanne, if I die, you'll sell everything and move to the Chain of Lakes.' You said 'Oh, no, that will never happen,' and here we are." I recalled that conversation very clearly. We had a good laugh over that one.

⁓✦⁓

In 2001, I went to two doctors concerning my sore hip, and they both told me that I needed hip replacement. I let it go in one ear and out the other; no way could I go through something like that.

In 2002, I was ready to face this serious operation. I did my homework and made the necessary arrangements.

I lined up a room at the nursing home for the month of August for rehabilitation. I checked into my insurance coverage and found out they would cover all of my expenses, including my nursing home stay. I was most grateful and counted my blessings during that adverse time.

On August 2, 2002, Julie and John came for my surgery. They stayed overnight in a hotel close to the hospital in Oshkosh.

When I woke up after my surgery, family members filled my room. Some stayed for hours just keeping a vigil while I slept. Though I dreaded this entire ordeal, the loving care of my family and friends saw me through to the end. I mended and healed in a proper manner.

One night, while in the nursing home, I woke up very hungry. I craved homemade peach jam. I loved to can, and I wished I was home canning jam. The next morning, at ten o'clock, in walked my friend Rosemary with a warm jar of freshly-canned peach jam. I opened it immediately, grabbed a roll I had put in my night stand from dinner and dipped it into the jam. Yummy!

At one point in my nursing home stay, my good friend, Inez, came and took me to lunch. After all, it was the month of August, and the town was booming with tourists, and everyone was having fun. She didn't like seeing me lying in the nursing home. I appreciated that so much, but I couldn't wait to get back into my comfort zone where I continued to mend and heal.

I returned to my home on Labor Day weekend. My son, John, and his family spent the weekend with me. Since my bedrooms were all on the upper level, I had a hospital bed placed in the middle of my dining room where my dining table once sat. Upon arriving to my home, my five-year old-grandson, Jack, looked up at the hanging light fixture above my bed and said, "Grandma, how come you're laying on the dining room table?"

Once my surgery was over, I didn't want to deal with the stairs anymore. Once again, I put my home up for sale. Wingspan sold very fast. The new owners allowed me to stay in my home until the first of the year in order to take the time I needed to heal from hip surgery and pack for my move to wherever I was headed.

I knew I wanted to build a condo on the golf course, but until the proper zoning went through, I had to wait. I was in limbo.

I was able to house sit for some friends, taking care of their pets while they left for Florida for six weeks. Then, my best friend, Karen, opened her home to me until my condo on the golf course was ready.

While the condo was being built, I went out to it every day. By this time, I had graduated to the cane, and I was on top of my game. I was excited to pick things out for my new dwelling.

I was able to move in on June 1, 2003. This was a happy time for me. I lived totally on my own and was getting used to it.

My new condo was beautiful, and I took my time having furniture refinished and couches and chairs recovered. I chose red as my primary furniture color, and I chose off white carpeting. The combination was stunning, and my new Pier I items—glass top dining table and end tables—enhanced the other décor.

During this time, I stayed home a lot and really settled into my new home. I made sure there was plenty of room for the children and grandchildren who came for frequent visits.

Though there were very few trees in this new subdivision, I was able to view the morning sunrises and evening sunsets without obstruction. It seemed like I could reach out and touch the Big Dipper at night. Cloud formations were in plain view all day long, and the thunder and lightning storms were to die for.

I would sit on my back deck on the Fourth of July and watch fireworks in every direction. For the next three years, almost all of my time was taken up with settling in my new digs. It had been nearly ten years since Wally died, and it was time to become content with what I had and to not dwell on what I didn't have.

I often went to my brother Billy's church in Plainfield, and I enjoyed his Sunday services. It was hunting season, and I asked Billy if he was going deer hunting. He said he couldn't even consider that sport until he had a heart valve repaired. I was surprised because that was the first I had heard of his problem.

On December 27, 2004, I was staying with my three nieces at their house in Plainfield. Billy went into surgery at 8:00 AM. We didn't hear anything until very late in the afternoon. By seven o'clock in the evening, Billy's wife, Julie, called to ask me if I could drive the children to Marshfield Hospital, which was about an hour away. She said Billy was still in surgery, and she was having a bad day.

We grabbed tooth brushes, threw on coats, and away we went. We got up to Marshfield Hospital at 8:00 PM. Billy had passed away five minutes earlier. Our family was devastated.

God called my youngest brother, Billy, home, and we had to accept that. Billy loved the Lord. In the midst of all the people who were gathered at that hospital waiting area, there were many tears, but there were also people praying out loud for God to comfort those of us whom Billy had left behind.

At least one thousand people attended Billy's funeral. We anticipated this crowd because we knew how many people Billy had led to the Lord. His funeral service was held at the Tri-County Auditorium in order to accommodate the gathering.

I was next to our dear mother, who just sat there, contemplating her thoughts. She was quiet and gentle spirited, and we were sad that she had to experience the death of her youngest son.

Many people came up to Mom during the visitation. I heard time and time again, "Mrs. Waters, if it weren't for your son, Billy, I wouldn't know the Lord." Our Mom would just nod her head and accept hugs of sympathy from Billy's friends.

Billy was buried on New Year's Eve in 2004. The start of 2005 was a sad time for the Waters family.

⸻

Meeting Bill Sund after being widowed for almost ten years started out as no big deal. I had just gotten settled in, and he never seemed to be a person that I would gravitate toward. However, I didn't know him very well. Whenever I would see Bill, he seemed so quiet. Bill turned out to be proof to me that again, you can't judge a book by its cover.

He sent a sympathy card to me when my brother, Billy, died. I had a stack of sympathy cards from friends in our town that had recently left for their winter homes down south. I went through these cards and wrote notes to some of them, thanking them for their concern and wishing them a nice season.

When I came to Bill Sund's card, I read it again. He said just the right words, and I was touched and set his note aside. I got to thinking about him a little later and wondered how he was doing since the death of his wife five months prior.

I called and left a message, thanking him for the sympathy note. He called me a couple of days later and referred me to a book that may be helpful for my sister-in-law in her grieving stages. The book, *A Grief Observed,* is by C.S. Lewis. I immediately went to the bookstore and purchased a copy. Again, I thought nothing of that phone contact with Bill.

He called again a week later and asked if I found the book. I just told him I had the book and wanted to read it before I passed it on. He said if I hadn't gotten it, he would have brought his copy to me.

During the second phone conversation, Bill asked me if I would like to go to a Jazz Mass at the Episcopal Church with him. It happened to be Super Bowl Sunday in the evening and I had been invited to a party at the Ryans's. It turned out that he was invited to the same party. We went to the Mass and the party together.

Oh boy! Then it started. We started talking about our past, growing up in neighboring towns and recalling all of the people that we both knew.

He was a football player for Neenah High, and I, being a cheerleader for St. Mary's in Menasha (a neighboring town), had so much to talk about. We found great company in each other and could chat for hours on end.

My doorbell would ring at seven o'clock in the morning, Bill would stick his head in the door, and in would bound Beau, his little white dog. Sometimes we would chat until noon.

I loved all of the commotion with the pets and our interaction. I especially loved that we were on the same page with our Christian walk. He was involved in weekly Bible studies, too. We both agreed that we were Christians first, and we just happened to belong to a certain denomination.

After about a year of seeing each other on a daily basis, I was at his house one Sunday for dinner and it began to snow pretty hard. It was after we had eaten dinner that he said, "Well, I guess you'll be spending the night." That didn't bother me, but after thinking about it, I proceeded to get my coat and tell him I was going home. No particular reason, I just didn't want to get farther into our relationship without a commitment. After all, I only lived five miles down the road, and the snow wasn't going to be a problem.

When I left that night, I knew his feelings were hurt, and I thought for sure he would call me to be sure I got home safely. He didn't. I thought that I had made a mistake. Why had I left such a fine guy? I didn't think I would ever hear from him again.

The next morning, I got on my treadmill and started a vigorous workout. The phone rang at eight o' clock in the morning, and it was Bill. My heart flipped. He asked if I wanted to go out for pizza that evening. I said that would be fine. We went for pizza, but somehow, things just weren't the same. We both seemed a little uneasy.

By Thursday, when I had not heard from him, I decided to call him and invite him to dinner. He graciously accepted. I made a special dinner of pork chops, home-made apple sauce, garlic smashed potatoes, a yummy salad, and cherry pie a la mode. Again, things seemed strained. He seemed rather distant to me.

I said I thought we were drifting apart. It didn't bother me too much. I had been there before and knew I would be okay if this didn't work out. He immediately said, "No, we aren't drifting apart because I want to ask you to marry me." I was so happy inside, and I am sure it showed. I said, "Wait a minute, did you just propose to me?" His reply was, "Yes, in my own way I did." Oh, my goodness! I was so happy, the happiest I had been in over ten years!

It was a no-brainer. I accepted Bill's proposal on the spot.

I had not met his children, and we had a lot of things to work out before we could proceed with our plans. He didn't want me to say anything to anybody for awhile, but little by little, he told my sister, Colleen, when she was visiting me one day, and soon afterwards, we told my best friend, Karen, about our plans.

During the months to follow, his family accepted me completely. My family loved Bill Sund right from the beginning, as well. Bill's father, Roy, was well known in the Fox Valley Area, and my family knew that Bill would be a good husband for me.

I left for Israel on May 8, 2006. While I was away, Bill kept busy by making plans for our honeymoon trip.

Here we are in a fishing boat on the Sea of Galilee, 2006
My sister, Colleen, Billy's wife Julie, me, and my sister Kathy
From the author's personal collection,

I really don't know where to start with this awesome trip to Israel. My brother, Billy, had been to Israel many times before he died, and he always wanted his sisters to go, too. Kathy, Colleen, and I joined Billy's wife, Julie, on this memorable two-week trip.

I loved my Bible, and it really came alive during and after our trip to Israel. We landed in Tel Aviv Airport after a very long flight. We were exhausted, but our first stop on the Mediterranean Sea opened our tired eyes, and from that time on things started happening. We stayed on the shores of the Sea of Galilee those first few nights. Imagine: we could walk in the footprints of Jesus.

Spending an entire morning in a fishing boat on the Sea of Galilee, not unlike the one Jesus and the Apostles occupied, soothed our souls. At one point, the captain stopped the engine so we could hear the quiet!

There wasn't a dry eye in the boat when they raised the Jewish Flag and sang their national anthem, followed by raising the American flag while we honored our country. I get goose bumps thinking about all of those events.

We had Bible studies at several sites along the tour, but the one that stands out in my mind was the singing of Christian songs beside the River Jordan while one of the gals played her guitar. We were all at peace with the world while we listened to the rushing waters by the river's edge. We stood at the place on the River Jordan where Jesus was baptized by John the Baptist.

We went from the Sea of Galilee to Bet She'an, Jericho, all the way to Eilat at the southern tip of Israel.

While in Eilat, we stopped at a diamond factory. I didn't need anything and I'm not a big diamond fan. However, when the sales woman approached me, I had a question for her. "Do you have any teardrop diamond earrings set in white gold?" She went right to my wedding earrings.

I wanted a bargain. After much consultation and a trip over to the manager, we could not agree on a price. Then I told her to tell her manager that these earrings would be worn by me at my upcoming wedding. He took one look at me, grinned, and just nodded his head yes. He probably thought if I could get married at that age, then I deserved those diamond earrings. The tour guide thanked all of us for making Israel a little greener that day.

Some of us experienced Baptism at Ein Gedi. It was

a very long walk almost straight up to the water fall, and when we arrived at the scene, it was well worth the climb.

It would take an entire book to describe this trip, but one event in particular rocked my world. When we entered the Tomb of the Rock, my sister-in-law, Julie, pointed out the spot that she had placed our brother Billy's ashes. It's a good thing we didn't have to read sheet music while we sang, because all three of us sisters were very emotional with this whole setting.

We spent the last five days and nights in Jerusalem, and it was an experience of a lifetime. I hope to elaborate on this in my next book.

Because the vegetation was so huge and lush, I foolishly asked our tour guide what kind of fertilizer they used. He kindly pulled me aside, put his arm around me, and said, "Suzy, I think you are missing something, here. You're in the land of milk and honey." Of course we were.

At midnight on the last night there, we left our hotel for our ride back to the airport. Our bus driver put a CD in, and we all sang along to "We're Walking on Holy Ground" and other spiritual songs.

August 26, 2006

Mr and Mrs. William P. Sund were joined
in marriage on August 26, 2006.
From the author's personal collection.

My best friend, Karen, helped me with all of my
wedding plans on the home front and stood by my side
throughout the ceremony. My daughter, Julie, was my
senior attendant and is to my left in the above picture. I
am very happy and blessed to be married to Bill Sund. He
was very instrumental in getting me back to writing my
story. He knows I have a message to pass along.

We enjoyed a wonderful Canadian honeymoon trip, a
cruise around the Thousand Islands. On our last night on
the cruise, the staff honored us with a cake, champagne,
and live music.

While packing up our items to exit the ship, I looked
at Bill and said, "I know we are going to enjoy every single
day, without any arguments, for the rest of our lives." His
response was, "Hey, wait a minute! Aren't we going to

live together?" We've had fun with that line over and over again.

A couple of years before Mom's passing; we noticed signs of her dementia. Through all of the years that our Mom was bringing up her children, she never lost her poise. She was always a classy lady, both mentally and physically.

The last time I brought her to my condo for a weekend visit, she was ninety years old. I did this periodically, and it was always fun to share weekends with my mom. During this particular visit, Mom had on a pair of fashionable, black ankle boots with a skinny, heel. I was afraid she would slip on my hardwood floors, so I brought out a pair of flat black loafers. She took one look at them and said, "Oh, no, that's not me." She walked around all weekend in those heeled boots. Like I said, she had class.

That said, it was extremely hard to see Mom lose touch with reality. Patti paved the way for Mom to enter into a wonderful facility in Neenah, Wisconsin. My sisters were with her almost every day those last couple of years. I knew she always had plenty of company, so I would visit about once a month. Each time I went, Mom became less and less interested in life, it seemed. She would just sit in her rocker and smile. Mom stopped talking altogether those last few months, but still she wore that eternal smile.

She loved to play rummy, so one day, Ruth (another resident), Mom, and I sat in the dining room of the Visiting Nurse Association (VNA) home playing rummy. Ruth said deuces were wild, but Mom just shook her head no. I thought, "No big deal, I'll just humor them, and we'll do the best they can." At one point, Ruth put down a deuce (2) and started to pick up Mom's trick. Mom yelled, "No!, No!, No," gave the deuce back to Ruth, and picked up the trick.

Mom passed away peacefully on January 4, 2008. Patti planned a wonderful funeral for her. Among the many tributes from my other siblings, I composed and read the following poem at Mom's funeral service.

A Tribute to My Mother,
Catherine Waters
By: Suzanne Waters-Sund, 1/4/2008

Christmas Eve 2006—Mom playing Christmas Carols for the family. *From the author's personal collection.*

Until We Meet Again

In the entire world, there's never been, a Mom quite like you;

You married Dad, and one year later there was Patti Lou.

In just fourteen months, Patti had a sister named Suzanne;

Jim couldn't wait to join us two, he said, "They need a man."

Margie and Frances didn't survive; they were numbers four and five;

Kathryn Ann was next in line, joining in to keep fun alive.

Then came Jeanne with the curly hair, she looked like a little toy!

When Chip was born, Jim said "Hurray! There's another boy!"

Doug surprised us all one day, and we thought he was the end;

But Colly Dolly said, "Hey, wait!" You need another
friend.

Our house was always rockin', and then Donny came a
knockin'.

Soon, Billy said, "Make room for me. Can I join your
family tree?"

I told you, Mom, and I'll say it times ten, you gave us all
so much back then.

We're going to miss you, dear Mother—but thanks for
giving us each other.

UNTIL WE MEET AGAIN!

I think we take turns in life. I took a turn with a
little happiness, some illness, and great sadness. However,
nothing gave me as much peace as getting familiar with
the Holy Bible, God, and His love for me. Now, it's my
turn to pass this information on.

The following are some remarkable instances that
took place once I opened my eyes and heart to my Lord
and Savior.

At one of our prayer meetings in our home in the
woods, I invited the people to be aware of the next week's
happenings. I asked them to be ready to share something
special that happened to them. We agreed to try to make a
difference in someone's life.

As the week continued, I went about my daily routine.
It was pouring rain. I lived ten miles out of town and
needed to do some errands. I had just turned onto the
highway when I noticed a car stranded off of the road on

my right. I looked in my rear view mirror as I passed and saw what I thought to be a man leaning over the car, under the hood.

I didn't have a car phone; hardly anyone did in the early eighties. I felt it was time to practice what I preached at our prayer meeting. I went back, rolled down my window and asked if the person needed help. It was a woman, and like me, she was skeptical. I said I lived down the road and would take her to my house to make a phone call for help. Again, she was hesitant. I told her that we had just had our weekly Bible study last night, and we vowed to make a difference in somebody's life this week. She chuckled and got in my car.

We introduced ourselves and had some small talk for awhile. She mentioned that she and her family had recently moved to the Waupaca area from the inner core of Milwaukee. I began to tell her about my teaching experiences at St. Gall's School. She said she went to St. Gall's School as a child. Now my wheels started turning. Between the time she got in my car and the time it took a service vehicle to get to her car, we discovered that she was *Pam*. I was her teacher's helper at St. Gall's School in the sixties. Talk about a miracle! Pam and I sat in the car with tears in our eyes, hugging each other and praising God. She was on her way to her new job in Waupaca when her car gave out! She said she often wondered why I never returned to help at her school. Boy, did I have a story to tell at our next prayer meeting!

After I accepted the Lord into my life, I was tossing and turning, half asleep in the middle of the night. I was trying to come up with an eight-digit Biblical saying for my car's license plate. I thought of John 3:16 first, followed by Phil 4:13, and a few other favorite passages from the Bible. I then thought, "Why am I doing this in the middle of the night? I need my sleep!" I turned over, glanced at the clock, and in big red numbers was my license plate message: 3:16. I called the license bureau that day. John 3:16 was taken, but I could get JO 3:16 which I did.

That license plate stayed with me, until I changed it to Psalm 15. That's a good message, too.

God shows his love in so many different ways. I had been laid up for nine weeks one time after I took a fall while shopping for flowers in a greenhouse. After a few weeks, I decided to try to take a walk down the highway where we lived. I had my cane and was walking slow when I started to pray that God would show me something special today. I was thanking Him for watching over me and helping my torn hamstring heal because the doctors were concerned about a blood clot developing.

It wasn't more than a minute later that I heard it! Knock, knock, knock! The loud, hollow sound startled me for a moment. I looked in the direction of the noise, and there it was: a pileated woodpecker. Wow! It was perched on the side of a tree with the sun shining through it to enhance those beautiful colors. Talk about God answering prayer! I couldn't thank Him enough.

It was the night before Thanksgiving. Weather people predicted a snowstorm. My son, John, stopped by MHCCW's Stevens Point office where I was working. He assured me that the weather was fine, and we both should be able to make it home before the storm.

It was dark when I left the office. Within five minutes, all I could see was the swirling snow in front of my headlights. I couldn't tell how the traffic was moving because I couldn't see the cars. I knew I was pointed in the eastern direction. All I could do was pray for guidance.

I saw a red, waving light ahead. I crawled along in the deep snow. The man waving the red light was standing next to his overturned semi that was blocking the highway. I rolled down my window, and amidst the howling wind I shouted that I didn't know where I was. As he guided me around this truck, his reply was fast and furious. "Ma'am, keep going straight ahead, and don't stop." I did what he said. I knew it would have been dangerous to stop because I would have gotten stranded big time.

Honestly, if I had seen a light in one of the farm houses that I knew were along that road, I would have pulled in one of those driveways, trudged through the deep snow to the house, pounded on the door, and asked to spend the night without any fear. I could picture myself doing that, but there were no lights to be seen in the driving snow.

I heard myself saying over and over, "Jesus, take the wheel and lead me home." I had a Christian station on the radio, and I was singing along to familiar tunes. That always seems to calm this Waters' girl.

When I could barely see the Ron and Lloyd's Grocery

Store sign, I carefully crept into the parking lot and went inside to call Wally and John. They were anxiously awaiting my arrival.

When the snow started with a vengeance, John said he turned around and was going to go back and get me, but he thought he saw me going east, so he followed that car for nearly twenty-five miles.

When I finally arrived home, we all embraced. Wally said, "Thanksgiving Day is tomorrow, but our thanksgiving starts now."

God is always with us. We just need to recognize this and call on Him in all situations.

This is my life from its beginning through September, 2010. It is not the end of my life. I thank God every day because when I was unable to help myself, He was there guiding and leading me through those tough times. Oh, yes, there may be more tough times, but I have learned to trust that if He brings me to it, He will help me through it.

I have a few more things I would like to share with you. Please read on.

PART IV

CHAPTER 23

AN INTRODUCTION TO THE SIXTY-SIX BOOKS OF THE HOLY BIBLE

(RE: PSALM 23)

I N December of 2005, I displayed posters around town and wrote a note in the newspaper. I was interested in getting people together and introducing them to the Holy Bible. Along with ten other people, we started a "Walk through the Bible" class. It took us five years, meeting for one hour each week, to go through the Bible while listening to and watching audio and video tapes of the Old Testament. The Bible contains awesome stories that start at the beginning of time.

Unless otherwise noted, all scripture quotes and introductions are taken from the New International Version of the Holy Bible (See above).

Genesis

Introduction:

The word genesis means "beginning." There are many beginnings in the Book of Genesis—the beginning of the universe, the beginning of man and woman, the beginning of human sin, the beginning of God's promises and plans for salvation, and the beginning of a special relationship between Abraham and God.

Genesis tells us about God's special people and His plan for their lives. Some of these people are Adam and Eve, Noah, Abraham, Isaac, Jacob (or Israel), and Joseph and his brothers.

Joseph's brothers are Reuben, Simeon, Levi, Judah, Issachar, Zebulun, Benjamin, Dan, Naphtali, Gad, and Asher. They make up the twelve tribes of Israel. They have one sister named Dinah.

Genesis is the first book in what is called the Pentateuch—a word that means five books and includes the first five books of the Bible.

These books are also known as the books of the law because they contain God's instructions and laws for the people of Israel. Genesis is included because it tells the history of how the Israelites became God's special people.

Outline of contents:

The Universe, the Earth, and Man (1:1–2:25)

Man's Fall and the Results of Sin (3:1–5:32)

The story of Noah (6:1–9:29)

The Scattering of the Human Race (10:1–11:32)

The Life of Abraham (12:1–25:18)

Isaac and His Family (25:19–26:35)
Jacob (Israel) and his Sons (27:1–37:1)
The Life of Joseph (37:2–50:26)

Exodus

Introduction:

Exodus means "exit" or "departure." The title of this book comes from one of the greatest miracles of God's care for His people in the Old Testament—the Israelites being freed from slavery and leaving Egypt.

Exodus continues the story of God's people, now called the Israelites. The story of the Israelites began with Abraham in Genesis.

From Moses' birth, God chose him for a special task—to lead the Israelites out of Egypt to Canaan, the land God had promised them. Moses is the main character and author of this book. Although he was weak in his own strength, God made him strong with his power and encouragement (7:6–11). God showed His power to the Israelites and the Egyptians in the ten plagues (7:14–11:10). The last plague made it possible for the Israelites to leave Egypt. Before leaving Egypt, they celebrated the Passover(chapter 12).

The Israelites began their journey protected and guided by God, who manifested in a pillar of cloud by day and a pillar of fire by night. With Moses leading them, they crossed the Red Sea and settled in the desert at the foot of Mt. Sinai for about one year. Here, God set up his covenant with the Israelites by giving them the laws for living and worshiping.

The covenant between God and Israel began a relationship in which Israel was identified as God's holy nation. God gave his people the Ten Commandments, priests, and a tabernacle to help them live lives that showed they were truly God's people.

Outline of contents:

Moses—God's Leader (1:1–4:31)
The Contest with Pharaoh (5:1–13:19)
From Egypt to Mt. Sinai (13:20–19:2)
God's Covenant and Laws (9:3–24:8)
The Tabernacle for Worship (24:9–40:38)

LEVITICUS

Introduction:

Leviticus means "about the Levites." The Levites were God's priests, and Leviticus contains many of the rules they needed to do their work—rules for worshiping God, making sacrifices, and handling everyday problems concerning cleanliness. Although many of the rules were given only for the Levites, the purpose of all the laws that were given was to help the Israelites worship and live as God's holy people. A key statement for the entire book is, "Be holy, because I am holy" (11:44–45)

Outline of contents:

The Laws and Instructions for Offerings (1:1–7:38)
Aaron and His Sons as God's Priests (8:1–10:20)
Rules for Holy Living (11:1–15:33)
The Day of Atonement (16:1–34)
Practical Holiness (17:1–22:33)
The Sabbath, Feasts, and Seasons (23:1–25:55)
Conditions for God's Blessings (26:1–27:34)

The text of the Holy Bible, *New Living Translation— Life Application Study Bible,* may be quoted in any form (written, visual, electronic or audio), up to the inclusive of two hundred and fifty (250) verses without express written permission of the publisher provided that the verses quoted do not account for more than twenty percent of the work in which they are quoted, and provided that a complete book of the Bible is not quoted.

Summary of the Book of Leviticus— *(LASB) Life Application Study Bible—New Living Translation*

"God seems so far away, if only I could see Him." Have you ever felt this way? Struggling with loneliness, burdened by despair, riddled with sin, overwhelmed by problems? Made in God's image, we were created to have a close relationship with him, and when fellowship is broken, we are incomplete and need restoration. Communion with the living God is the essence of worship. It is vital, touching the very core of our lives. Perhaps this is why a whole book of the Bible is dedicated to worship. After Israel's dramatic exit from Egypt, the nation was camped at the foot of Mt. Sinai for two years to listen to God (Exodus 19–Numbers 10). It was a time of resting, teaching, building, and meeting with him. Redemption in Exodus is the foundation for cleansing, worship, and service in Leviticus.

The overwhelming message of Leviticus is the holiness of God. "You must be holy because I, the Lord your God, am holy" (19:2). How can an unholy people approach a Holy God? Answer: sin must be dealt with! Thus, the opening chapters of Leviticus give detailed instruction for offering sacrifices, which were the active symbols of repentance and obedience. Whether bulls, grains, goats, or sheep, the sacrificial offerings had to be perfect, with no defects or bruises—pictures of the ultimate sacrifice to come, Jesus the Lamb of God. Jesus came and opened the way to God by giving up his life as the final sacrifice in our place. True worship and oneness with God begins as we confess our sin and accept Christ as the only one who can redeem us from sin and help us approach God.

In Leviticus, sacrifices, priests, and the sacred Day of Atonement opened the way for the Israelites to come to God. God's people were also to worship him with their lives. Thus, we read of Purity Laws in chapters 11–15, we read of rules for daily living concerning family responsibilities, sexual conduct, relationships, and worldliness in chapters 18–20, we read of vows in chapter 27. These instructions involve one's holy walk with God, and the patterns of spiritual living still apply today.

The final emphasis in Leviticus is celebration. The book gives instructions for the feasts. These were special, regular, and corporate occasions for remembering what God had done, giving thanks to him, and rededicating our lives to his service (23)

Our Christian traditions and holidays are different, but they are necessary ingredients of worship. We, too, need special days of worship and celebration with our brothers and sisters in Christ to remember God's goodness in our lives.

As you read Leviticus, rededicate yourself to holiness, worshiping God in private confession, public service, and group celebration.

Purpose: Leviticus is a handbook for priests and Levites outlining their duties in worship and a guidebook of holy living for the Hebrews.

Author: Moses

Dates of Events: 1445–1444 BC

Setting: At the foot of Mt. Sinai. God is teaching the Israelites how to live as holy people.

Special feature: Holiness is mentioned 152 times, more than in any other Book of the Bible.

NUMBERS

Introduction:

Numbers gets its name from the two accounts in chapters 1 and 26 of the numbering or counting of the people of Israel. Moses is the author as well as the leader of the Israelites.

The first part of the book tells about Israel's year while camped at the foot of Mount Sinai.

The second part of the book tells of the journey of Israel from Mt. Sinai to the east side of the Dead Sea.

The third part of the book tells of the preparations for entering and conquering Canaan.

Throughout the thirty-eight years of wandering in the desert, one thing became clear to Israel: God's constant care for them. He miraculously supplied the Israelites with manna, water, and quails for their forty years in the desert. God loved and forgave his people continually, even though they rebelled against Him and their leaders.

Outline of contents:

Instructions for Camping and Marching (1:1–10:10)
From Sinai to the Plains of Moab (10:11–21:35)
Balaam, Balak, and Israel (22:1–25:18)
Instructions for Conquest and Possession of the Land of Canaan (26:1–36:13)

DEUTERONOMY

Introduction:

Deuteronomy means "Second Law." After forty years, the Israelites were about to enter the Promised Land of Canaan. Before they did, Moses wanted to remind them of their history, all that God had done for them, and the laws they had to continue to obey as God's chosen people.

His first speech reminded the people of God's goodness to them through their journey and his giving them the land of Canaan. Moses' second speech was a summary of God's laws, including the Ten Commandments. Moses told the people to "love the Lord your God with all your heart and with all your soul and with all your strength" 6:5, in order to continue to enjoy God's blessings. Moses also emphasized that to keep their relationship right with God; the people had to teach their children to love the Lord and to obey his commandments.

Deuteronomy ends with the people of Israel being reminded of the covenant God had made with them (29), Joshua's appointment to be the new leader (31), and Moses' death (34).

Outline of contents:

Moses' First Speech: Israel's History (1:1–4:43)

Moses' Second Speech: Review of the Law (4:44–11:32)

Rules for Daily Living (12:1–26:19)

The Results of Obedience and Disobedience (27:1–28:68)

The Renewal of the Covenant (29:1–30:20)

Moses' Blessing on Israel and His Death (31:1–34:12)

Suzanne's note: Keep in mind that Moses, though he was a favorite of the Lord's, was still a human being and prone to error.

JOSHUA

Introduction:

This book has the name of its leading character as its title. Joshua had been chosen and appointed by God just before Moses' death.

Joshua is the story of both Joshua and Israel as they, with God's help, conquered the Promised Land, Canaan. The people miraculously crossed the River Jordan and conquered the town of Jericho. Then, with God's help again, they quickly took possession of all the main areas of Canaan.

Before Joshua died, he reminded the people of God's covenant promises to them. He instructed his people to keep on loving and obeying God. Publicly, he spoke of his own willingness to serve God when he said, " ... choose for yourselves this day whom you will serve, But as for me and my household, we will serve the Lord" (24:15).

Outline of Contents:

Preparation for Possession of Canaan (1:1–5:15)
The Conquest of Canaan (6:1–12:24)
The Division of the Land by Tribes (13:1–21:45)
Farewell and Death of Joshua (22:1–24:33)

JUDGES

Introduction:

This book tells of Israel's history for the period between the death of Joshua and the ministry of Samuel. This time period was known for its heroes—called judges—who ruled the tribes of Israel.

The events in Judges followed a certain pattern:

1. The Israelites lived in peace while serving and loving God.
2. The Israelites forgot God and worshiped idols.
3. God punished his people by sending a neighboring nation to fight and rule over them.
4. The Israelites turned to God and asked for forgiveness.
5. God forgave his people and sent a judge to help conquer their enemy.

This pattern of events repeated itself many times during this time period in Israel's history.

A total of fifteen judges are listed. The best-known judges are Deborah, Gideon, and Samson.

Outline of Contents:

Conditions During the Time of Judges (1:1–3:6)
Conquering Nations and Ruling Judges (3:7–16:31)
Idolatry and Civil War (17:1–21:25)

RUTH

Suzanne's Note: This is such a great story. I love Boaz for his respect and kindness to Ruth. I especially loved the end of the last chapter, 4:18–22. This is the family line from Perez to David: Perez, Hezron, Ram, Amminadab, Nahshon, Salmon, Boaz (Ruth's husband), Obed (son of Boaz and Ruth), Jesse (grandson of Ruth and father of David), David (the youngest of Jesse's eight sons). Once I read about Jesse and David, I felt a little closer to Mary, Joseph, and Jesus.

Introduction:

This book is named after the leading character whose story is told here. It may have been written during the reign of David, whose ancestry is traced in the final verses to his great-grandfather, Boaz, whose wife was Ruth.

Ruth tells the story of an Israelite couple who moved to Moab during a famine in Canaan. The husband and his two sons died, leaving the mother, Naomi, alone with her two daughters-in-law, Orpah and Ruth. Naomi decided to move back to Israel, and Ruth insisted on going back with her. Back in Israel, they looked to their relative Boaz for help, and Ruth finally married Boaz. From their family came the royal family of David and the Messiah, Jesus Christ.

This book teaches us much about love and devotion. It also teaches us of God's concern for our everyday needs and that he is working out his plan for salvation.

Outline of Contents:

Naomi's Departure from Israel and Her Return (1:1–22)
Ruth's Welcome (2:1–3:18)
Boaz and Ruth (4:1–22)

1 Samuel

Introduction:

1 Samuel records the lives of Samuel and Saul and much of the life of David. First Samuel begins with the birth of Samuel and his training in the temple. It describes how he led Israel as prophet, priest, and judge.

When the people of Israel demanded a king, Samuel, by God's leading, anointed Saul to be the first king of Israel. But Saul was disobedient to God, and God rejected him as king. Then, Samuel secretly anointed David to take Saul's place. The struggles between Saul and David make up the rest of this book. Although we learn much of these people's disobedience, there is a stronger emphasis on their goodness and obedience to God.

It was during this part of Israel's history that the nation changed from having judges as leaders to having a king as their neighboring nations had. Samuel, as prophet, priest, and judge, had a great deal of influence throughout this time period.

Outline of Contents:

Eli as Priest and Judge (1:1–4:22)
Samuel as Leader of Israel (5:1–8:22)
Saul, the First King of Israel (9:1–15:35)
David and Saul (16:1–30:31)
Death of Saul (31:1–13)

2 Samuel

Introduction:

2 Samuel continues the story of the beginning of Israel's kingdom. It starts with Saul's death. Then, it describes David's forty-year reign. Some of the best-known stories are the capture of Jerusalem, David's sin with Bathsheba, and Absalom's rebellion.

Outline of Contents:

David as King of Judah (1:1–4:12)
David Unites Israel (5:1–24:25)

1 Kings

Introduction:

Beginning with Solomon's reign (about 971 BC), 1 Kings records the history of Israel through the divided kingdom to the death of Ahaziah, the son of Ahab. Chapters 3–11 describe Solomon's reign, including the building of the temple and the palace in Jerusalem.

Rehoboam, Solomon's son, took the throne after Solomon's death but lost the northern part of the kingdom to Jeroboam. After this, the northern kingdom was known as Israel, and the southern kingdom was called Judah. The last chapters of 1 Kings tell about the evil King Ahab and God's prophet Elijah, who condemned Ahab's wickedness and Israel's disobedience.

Because the author of First and Second Kings was interested in Israel's faithfulness to God and his covenant, he wrote about each king showing how he or she was faithful or unfaithful to God. The author often used the phrase, "did what was right in the eyes of the Lord," or "did evil in the eyes of the Lord," to describe the goodness or wickedness of the king.

Like *Judges*, the author records that when Israel was obedient, God brought peace to the land, but when the people were disobedient and worshiped idols, the land of Israel suffered wars and other disasters.

Outline of Contents:

The Reign of Solomon (1:1–11:43)
Rehoboam and Jeroboam (12:1–14:31)
Kings of Israel and Judah (15:1–16:34)
Elijah and Ahab (17:1–19:21)
The Reign of Ahab and Jezebel (20:1–22:53)

Suzanne's note: Out of those twenty kings, there were only nine who did what was right in the Lord's eyes: kings Asa, Jehoshaphat, Jehu (Israel), Joash, Amaziah, Azariah, Jotham, Hezekiah, and Josiah. All but Jehu were from Judah.

The longest reigning king, King Azariah of Judah, reigned for fifty-two years, and he was a good king, but the Lord afflicted him with leprosy. He did not remove the high places and the people continued to burn incense and offer sacrifices (2 Kings 15:1–7).

The shortest reigning king, King Zimri of Israel, reigned for seven days, and he did evil in the eyes of the Lord (1 Kings 16:15–20).

2 Kings

Introduction:

2 Kings continues the stories of the great prophets Elijah and Elisha. It also tells the history of the northern kingdom of Israel and the southern kingdom of Judah until they were both finally conquered. Israel was conquered by Assyria in 722 BC, and Judah was conquered by the Babylonians in 586 BC. In both kingdoms, God's prophets continually warned the people that God would punish them if they did not repent from their sins.

Outline of Contents:

Elijah and Elisha (1:1–8:15)
Kings of Israel and Judah (8:16–17:6)
Israel Taken Captive to Assyria (17:7–41)
Judah Survives Assyrian Rule (18:1–23:37)
Judah Taken Captive to Babylonia (24:1–25:30)

1 Chronicles

Suzanne's note:

Chronicle (n): an historical record.
Chronicle (v): to tell the history of.

Introduction:

Although the books of Chronicles seem like a repeat of Samuel and Kings, they are not. The Chronicles were written for the exiles who had returned to Israel after the Babylonian captivity to remind them they were from the royal line of David and were God's chosen people. The main theme is that God is always faithful to his covenant.

For these reasons, 1 Chronicles begins with an outline of history from Adam through the death of King Saul. The rest of the book is about the reign of King David. These books serve as both a warning and encouragement to the Jews to be faithful to the covenant.

Outline of Contents:

List of Generations (1:1–9:44)
The Reign of David (10:1–29:30)

2 CHRONICLES

Introduction:

2 Chronicles continues the history of David's royal line. Chapters 1–9 describe the building of the temple during Solomon's reign. Chapters 10–36 follow the history of the southern kingdom of Judah to the final destruction of Jerusalem and the people being taken captive to Babylon.

This book, like 1 Chronicles, shows that the people's relationship to God was most important. When the author wrote about the kings, he measured them on the basis of their faithfulness to God. The reigns of evil kings are reported by the author quickly, while the reigns of good kings are described in more detail.

Outline of Contents:

Ezra

Suzanne's note: Chapter 10 is especially noteworthy for "The People's Confession of Sin." Ezra (the priest) dealt with those who had taken wives from foreign lands.

Introduction:

The Book of Ezra tells about the return of the Jews from exile in Babylon. It begins in 539 BC with the decree of Cyrus, king of Persia, which allowed the people to go back to Jerusalem under the leadership of Zerubbabel. The people enthusiastically began rebuilding the temple and resumed sacrifices. However, for eighteen years, they were delayed by their enemies from the north. Finally, in 521 BC, a decree from Darius, king of Persia, let them finish. The people completed and dedicated the temple in 515 BC.

In 458 BC, Ezra, the priest, returned to Jerusalem with another group of Babylonian exiles. He taught the people the law and reformed their religious lives so the other nations around them could see that they were God's chosen nation.

Ezra is the author of the books of Ezra and Nehemiah.

Outline of Contents:

The First Exiles Return to the Land of Judah (1:1–2:70)
The Temple is Rebuilt (3:1–6:22)
Ezra's Return and Ministry (7:1–10:44)

NEHEMIAH

Introduction:

Nehemiah continues the history of the Jews who returned from exile in Babylon. Nehemiah gave up his job as cupbearer to Artaxerxes, the Persian king, to become governor of Jerusalem. Nehemiah went to Jerusalem in 444 BC, almost one hundred years after the return of the first exiles. Nehemiah led the people in repairing the walls of Jerusalem, and Ezra provided leadership for the people. An important part of this book is the description of the importance of prayer to Nehemiah.

Outline of Contents:

Nehemiah Rebuilds the Walls (1:1–7:3)
Change under Ezra (7:4–10:39)
Nehemiah's Plans (11:1–13:31)
Suzanne's notes: Chapter 11—The New Residents of Jerusalem. It tells of all the descendants of Judah, and it tells of Benjamin. It also lists who were the priests, Levites, and Gatekeepers.

Chapter 12—This Chapter lists the Priests and Levites who returned to Jerusalem. Verse 27 is the Dedication of the Wall of Jerusalem. Verse 30 reads, "When the priests and Levites had purified themselves ceremonially, they purified the people, the gates and the walls." Verse 40 tells how "the two choirs gave thanks then took their places in the house of God … "

Notice the last sentence in 12:43: "The sound of rejoicing in Jerusalem could be heard far away."

Again, we must remember all of these things, rituals, etc., took place in the Old Testament (before Christ).

At the very end of the Book of Nehemiah, note in Chapter 13 where Nehemiah says, "Remember me with favor, O my God."

Esther

Suzanne's note: Mordecai was the cousin and guardian of Esther. You will recall that after Esther's father and mother died (apparently she was a young girl), her cousin Mordecai took her in and raised her as his own daughter. Esther's real name was Hadassah (2:7).

Introduction:

The setting for the book of Esther is Susa, the Persian capital, during the time of Xerxes, who ruled Persia from 486–465 BC. The book tells the story of a beautiful Jewish girl whom King Xerxes chose to be his queen. When Haman plotted to murder all of the Jews, Queen Esther's cousin Mordecai persuaded Esther to try to save her people. Risking her own life, Esther appealed to the king and rescued the Jews.

Although the name of God does not appear in this book, his care for his chosen people is clearly shown. This exciting story of the rescue of the Jews is celebrated annually during the Feast of Purim, at which time the book of Esther is read aloud.

Suzanne's note: Purim is the feast or festival celebrated by the Jews to commemorate their deliverance from Haman. It is called the Feast of Lots because Haman tried to fix by lots the day on which the Jews were to be slain. It was celebrated on the fourteenth and fifteenth day of the Jewish month Adar (March).

Outline of Contents:

Job

Suzanne's note: Note in 1:6 where Satan confronted the Lord about Job, who had everything. The Lord finally lets Satan put Job to the test, and the rest is history.

Introduction:

The book of Job is named for its main character, a righteous man who was very rich. Even after losing everything he owned and suffering from a terrible sickness, Job still confessed his love for God.

The book questions the reasons for suffering, especially the suffering of people who love God and are good. Job's friends insisted he was suffering as punishment for his sins; Job defended himself by insisting that he had done nothing wrong to deserve this and expressed his trust in God.

Then God spoke and showed his mighty power. Job finally admitted that God is too great and wonderful for us to understand.

Outline of Contents:

Setting and Background (1:1–3:26)
Job's Discussions with Three Friends (4:1–31:40)
How is God Related to Job's Suffering? (4:1–14:22)
Do Wicked People Always Suffer? (15:1–21:34)
Is Job Guilty of Secret Sins? (22:1–31:40)

Elihu's Speech (32:1–37:24)

God Speaks (38:1–41:34)

The Lord Affords Job More Than He Had Before (42:1–17)

Suzanne's note: the book of Job is a great book in that it tells of the frailties of humans and the reality that human suffering, pain, and loss can lead us to coming close to blaming God. Job stood firm in his stance with God, and he deals with his friends' criticism in different ways.

PSALMS

Introduction:

Psalms is a collection of poems and songs of praise, worship, thankfulness, and repentance, and each one of them is complete by itself. They also show a variety of feelings, emotions, attitudes, and interests.

Of the one hundred fifty Psalms, one hundred of them are thought to be written by the following authors: David, seventy-three; Asaph, twelve; Sons of Korah, 10; Moses, one; Heman the Ezrahite, 1; Ethan the Ecrahite, one; and Solomon, one or two. The rest of the Psalms have no recorded author.

Because Psalms is written by so many people from different times, and because the psalms show such a variety of emotions, they have had a worldwide appeal and are familiar and loved by many people.

Hebrew poetry often uses pairs of lines. The second line either repeats the thought of the first or gives an opposite thought. Look for these pairs of lines as you read the Psalms.

Outline of Contents:

Book 1: Psalms 1–41
Book II: Psalms 42–72
Book III: Psalms 73–89
Book IV: Psalms 90–106
Book V: Psalms 107–150

Proverbs

Introduction:

Proverbs is a collection of wise sayings and good advice for daily living. The book begins by reminding us that "The fear of the Lord is the beginning of knowledge" (1:7). The first four chapters go on to discuss the importance of wisdom.

Following this, the author includes a collection of short and powerful two-line sayings that cover many different subjects including marriage, social behavior, friendship, justice, folly, poverty, wealth, family, love, laziness, and warnings against drinking and adultery.

Many of these proverbs came from King Solomon. Others were copied by the men of Hezekiah. Agur and Lemuel wrote the last two chapters.

Outline of Contents:

Instructions on Wisdom and Foolishness (1:1–9:18)
The Proverbs of Solomon (10:1–52:16)
Sayings of the Wise (22:17–23:34)
More Proverbs of Solomon (25:1–29:27)
Sayings of Ague and Lempel (30:1–31:31)
Suzanne's note: Wally loved Proverb 27:15–16. ☺ "A quarrelsome wife is like a constant dripping on a rainy day, restraining her is like restraining the wind or grasping oil with the hand."

Ecclesiastes

Introduction:

Ecclesiastes studies the meaning of life. The Teacher looks at wisdom, pleasure, work, power, riches, religion, and other things. All of these have some value and are useful in the proper time and place, but they have lasting value only if God is at the center of man's life. Reverence and respect for God and a real devotion in serving God are most important in making life have meaning. Without God, the Teacher says, "Everything is meaningless."

Outline of Contents:

Song of Songs

Introduction:

Although some scholars view Song of Songs as being a picture of Christ's love for his people, the more accepted view of Song of Songs is that it is a collection of love poems between a lover and his beloved. It is a beautiful picture of ideal human love and marriage.

Outline of Contents:

The Bride and the Bridegroom (1:1–2:7)
The Praise of her Beloved (2:8–3:5)
In Praise of the Bride (3:6-5:1)
A Troubled Love (5:2–7:9)
The Unbroken Communion (7:10–8:14)

Isaiah

Introduction:

Isaiah prophesied in Judah during the reigns of kings Uzziah, Jotham, Ahaz, and Hezekiah. According to tradition, Isaiah was martyred under Manasseh, the wicked son of Hezekiah, in about 680 BC.

Isaiah repeatedly warned the people that Jerusalem and Judah would be judged because of their wickedness. In chapter 39, he predicted the Babylonian exile. He also held to the hope that the kingdom would be restored.

Beginning in chapter 40, Isaiah offered comfort with the promises from God that (1) the Babylonian exiles would be allowed to return to Jerusalem, (2) a righteous, suffering servant (Jesus) would bring salvation, and (3) God would set up a new and righteous kingdom.

Outline of Contents:

Suzanne's note: Pay special attention to Isaiah 7:14. "Therefore the Lord himself will give you a sign: The Virgin will be with child and will give birth to a son, and will call him Immanuel." Immanuel means "God with us."

JEREMIAH

Introduction:

Jeremiah, like Isaiah, was a young man called by God to warn Judah about its wickedness. He spent the first twenty-five years of his ministry under Josiah, a good king who tried to bring the people of Judah back to God. After this, Jeremiah was often in danger from political and religious leaders who were angry because of his messages. Through all of this, God protected Jeremiah so he could continue to warn the wicked and comfort those who trusted in God.

After Jerusalem was destroyed in 586 BC, Jeremiah chose to remain with the people and eventually went with them to Egypt.

Since the messages of Jeremiah are not arranged in chronological order, it is helpful to read the history of Judah as found in Kings and Chronicles to better understand Jeremiah's messages.

Outline of Contents:

The Call of Jeremiah (1:1–19)
The Sinful Condition of Judah (2:1–6:30)
The Temple, the Law, and the Covenant (7:1–12:17)
The Certainty of Captivity (13:1–18:23)

Jeremiah Confronts the Leaders (19:1–29:32)
The Promise of Restoration (30:1–33:26)
The Kingdom Falls Apart (34:1–39:18)
The Trip to Egypt (40:1–45:5)
Message Concerning Foreign Nations
(46:1–51:64)
The Fall of Jerusalem (52:1–34)

Lamentations

Introduction:

The title of the book means "funeral songs." The author was probably Jeremiah, and he was grieving about the destruction of Jerusalem.

In the original language, Hebrew, the twenty-two verses in each of chapters 1, 2, and 4 use twenty-two letters of the Hebrew alphabet to start the verse. The third chapter has sixty-six verses, and every third verse starts with a new letter of the Hebrew alphabet. This is called an acrostic.

Here, Jeremiah reflects on the total destruction that has happened to Jerusalem and the Temple. He recognizes that all of this is the judgment of a righteous God. Knowing that God is merciful, he appeals for mercy in prayer to God.

Outline of Contents:

Jerusalem's Total Destruction (1:1–1:22)
God's Anger—Search for Comfort (2:1–2:22)
Thoughts on Suffering—Hope in God (3:1–3:66)
The Old Glory of Jerusalem—Present Misery (4:1–4:22)
A Prayer for God's mercy (5:1–5:22)

EZEKIEL

Introduction:

This book is named after the prophet Ezekiel, whose name means "God is strong." His messages are dated in the years between 593 and 571 BC, and they were given to his fellow exiles in Babylonian captivity.

Born in 623 BC to a priestly family, Ezekiel grew up in the surroundings of the temple in Jerusalem. In 597 BC, he was included in the exile to Babylon. In 593 BC, God called Ezekiel to be a prophet.

During the first part of his ministry, Ezekiel proclaimed basically the same message given by Jeremiah: Jerusalem and the temple were doomed to destruction because of the sinfulness and idolatry of the people.

After the news that Jerusalem actually had been destroyed in 586 BC reached Babylon, Ezekiel proclaimed a new message of hope and restoration. God would regather the Israelites from the ends of the earth and reestablish them in their own land. The nations who challenged Israel's return would be defeated and judged.

Outline of Contents:

Ezekiel's Call (1:1–3:27)
Jerusalem's Sinful Condition and Doom (4:1–24:27)
Foreign Nations in Prophecy (25:1–32:32)
Hopes for Restoration (33:1–39:29)
Israel Restored to Palestine (40:1–48:35)

Daniel

Introduction:

Daniel is the traditionally held author of this book. The entire book tells of the experiences of Daniel and his friends and the divine revelation that came to Daniel in dreams and visions during his lifetime, spanning about 605—530 BC.

Daniel was taken hostage from Jerusalem to the Babylonian court in 605 BC. After telling and interpreting King Nebuchadnezzar's dream, he was given a position of power. He wrote this book during Israel's captivity to encourage the people to trust in God, who controls all of history.

In the last six chapters of this book, Daniel describes his visions of the rise and fall of earthly kingdoms and finally the rise of an everlasting kingdom.

Outline of Contents:

Events During Nebuchadnezzar's Reign (1:1–4:37)
The Writing on the Wall (5:1–30)
Daniel in the Lions Den (5:31–6:28)
Visions During Belshazzar's Reign (7:1–8:27)
Daniel's Prayer and the Seventy "Sevens" (9:1–27)
Daniel's Final Revelation (10:1–12:13)

Hosea

Introduction:

The prophet Hosea was a citizen of the Northern Kingdom, which he commonly called Ephraim. He probably began his ministry before King Jeroboam II died in 753 BC, and he may have given his messages shortly before the fall of Samaria in 722 BC.

Chapters 1–3 tell about Hosea's love for his unfaithful wife, Gomer. Her unfaithfulness is a picture of Israel's unfaithfulness in its covenant relationship with God. Instead of responding in thankfulness and love to God for all of their blessings, the Israelites used their crops as offerings to idols. The injustice and mistreatment of others reflected their lack of love for God as well as for their fellow citizens.

Outline of Contents:

Hosea's Experience in Family Life (1:1–3:5)
Israel's Sin (4:1–6:3)
Punishment for Israel (6:4–10:15)
God's Judgment and Mercy (11:1–14:9)

Joel
(NIV Study Bible—same rights apply)

Introduction:

The prophet Joel cannot be identified with any of the twelve other figures in the Old Testament who have the same name. He is not mentioned outside the books of Joel and Acts (Acts 2:16). The nonbiblical legends of him are unconvincing. His father, Pathuel (1:1), is also unknown. Judging from his concern with Judah and Jerusalem (see 2:32; 3:1, 6, 8, 16–20), it seems likely that Joel lived in that area.

The book of Joel has striking linguistic parallels to the language of Amos, Micah, Zephaniah, Jeremiah, and Ezekiel. Some scholars maintain that the prophets borrowed phrases from one another; others hold that they drew more or less from the religious literary traditions that they and their readers shared in common.

Joel sees a massive locust plague and calls on everyone to repent: old and young (1:2–3), drunkards (1:5), farmers (1:11), and priests (1:13). He describes the locusts as the Lord's army and sees in their coming a reminder that the day of the Lord is near. He does not voice the popular notion that the day will be one of judgment on the nations but deliverance and blessings for Israel. Instead, with Israel (2:10–21), Jeremiah (4:5–9), Amos (5:18–20), and Zephaniah (1:7–18), he describes the day as one of punishment for an unfaithful Israel, as well. Restoration and blessing will come only after judgment and repentance.

Outline of Contents:

I. Title (1:1)

II. Judah experiences a foretaste of the day of the Lord (1:2–2:17)

    A. call to mourning and prayer (1:2–14)

    B. The announcement of the day of the Lord. (1:15–2:11)

    C. A call to repentance and prayer (2:12–17)

III. Judah is assured of salvation in the day of the Lord (2:18–3:21)

    A. the Lord's restoration of Judah (2:18–27)

    B. The Lord's renewal of His people (2:28–32)

    C. The coming of the day of the Lord. (3)

        1. The nations judged (3:1–16)

        2. God's people blessed (3:17–21)

Amos

Introduction:

The author's name, Amos, means "burden" or "burden bearer." Amos was a shepherd called by God to be a prophet in the northern cities of Israel during a time of riches and wealth for the northern kingdom.

He announced God's judgment on the people for turning away from God, for being cruel to the poor, and for living selfishly. In a series of five visions, Amos saw the day of doom as being close at hand. He warned the people that they were to prepare to meet God. For those who loved God, however, Amos had a word of hope. The day was coming when the kingdom of David would be reestablished, and God's people would dwell in safety.

Outline of Contents:

Judgment on Israel's Neighbors (1:1–2:5)
Judgment on Israel (2:6–16)
Israel's Guilt (3:1–6:14)
The Five Visions (7:1–9:10)
Israel's Restoration (9:11–15)

OBADIAH

Suzanne's note: This is the shortest book in the Old Testament, consisting of only one chapter.

The name Obadiah means "servant of Jehovah." Nothing more is known about this prophet than this short book containing his prophecy.

Obadiah is a book of prophecy against the nation of Edom. This country had invaded and plundered Jerusalem at least four times, so Obadiah announced God's judgment against them and prophesied that their kingdom would be destroyed.

The Edomites are never mentioned after the destruction of Jerusalem in 70 AD.

Outline of Contents:

The Doom of Edom (1–14)
Edom in the Day of the Lord (15–21)

JONAH

Introduction:

Jonah was a prophet whom God called to preach in the foreign city of Nineveh. Jonah tried to run away from God and was swallowed by a great fish.

When the fish returned him to land, Jonah went to Nineveh and warned the people about God's judgment. Jonah learned, to his dismay, that God would forgive even a heathen city if the people were sorry for their sins.

Outline of Contents:

Jonah Flees from the Lord (1:1–17)
Jonah's Prayer and Deliverance (2:1–10)
Jonah Goes to Nineveh (3:1–10)
Jonah's Anger at the Lord's Mercy (4:1–11)

MICAH

Introduction:

This book contains the writings of the prophet, Micah, who lived in the countryside of Judah during the reigns of Jotham, Ahaz, and Hezekiah. Micah warned about God's judgment against the capital cities of both kingdoms, Jerusalem and Samaria, because of the sinfulness of their rulers, prophets, and priests. The poor were oppressed, and people's lives did not show that they belonged to a holy God.

But Micah promised the restoration of Zion and a kingdom of peace for those who trusted in God. He prophesied that a ruler (Jesus Christ) born in Bethlehem would set up a kingdom that would last forever.

Outline of Contents:

Judgment against Samaria and Jerusalem (1:1–16)
Leaders Guilty of Oppression (2:1–3:12)
Divine Restoration (4:1–5:15)
Judgment and Mercy (6:1–7:20)

Nahum

Introduction:

Nahum was a prophet in the last half of the seventh century BC. He prophesied at the same time as Zephaniah, Jeremiah, and Habakkuk.

Nahum is a book of prophecy against Nineveh, the capital of Assyria. The prophet describes the cruelty of the Assyrians as they conquered nation after nation. He predicts the siege and destruction of Nineveh and the end of the kingdom of Assyria.

Nahum's only advice to Judah was that they observe their religious feasts, since the Assyrians would never again threaten Jerusalem.

Outline of Contents:

The Lord's Anger against Nineveh (1:1–15)
Nineveh's Fall (2:1–13)
Misery to Nineveh (3:1–19)

HABAKKUK

Introduction:

Habakkuk was written as a dialogue or conversation between God and the prophet. Habakkuk saw the leaders in Judah were oppressing the poor, so he asked the question as to why God allowed those wicked people to prosper. When God told him that the Babylonians would come to punish Judah, Habakkuk became more concerned. He did not understand how God could use the Babylonians, who were actually more wicked than the wicked Jews, to bring judgment on God's chosen people. God's answer was that the just would live by faith in God and that they had the assurance that God was doing what was right. God told Habakkuk that in due time, the Babylonians, too, would be judged and that justice would come about for the people of God. Habakkuk ends his book with a prayer of praise.

Outline of Contents:

Habakkuk's Question and God's Answer (1:1–11)
Habakkuk's Second Question and God's Answer (1:12–2:20)
Habakkuk's Prayer (3:1–19)

ZEPHANIAH

Introduction:

Zephaniah's ministry is dated in the reign of Josiah, 640–609 BC. He warned that the day of the Lord would bring judgment on Judah and Jerusalem, and he called the Jews to return to God.

Zephaniah then predicted that Judah's neighboring nations would be destroyed as well. With a note of hope, he promised that God would bring his people home.

Outline of Contents:

God's Judgment Announced (1:1–2:3)
Judgment against the Nations (2:4–15)
The Future of Jerusalem (3:1–20)

Haggai

Introduction:

Eighteen years had passed since Cyrus's decree in 538 BC had allowed the Jews to return from exile to Jerusalem. Because they were busy building their own homes, the people still had not finished building God's temple.

Haggai's message was that the time had come to build the house of the Lord. Under the leadership of Zerubbabel and Joshua, and with Haggai's prodding, the temple was rebuilt during the years 520–515 BC. Haggai told the people that the glory of the temple they were building would be greater than that of the former temple, even though the building itself would be less to look at. This temple would be greater because God would fill this house with his glory.

Outline of Contents:

ZECHARIAH

Introduction:

Zechariah's prophecies began two months after Haggai's first message in 520 BC. In his opening message, Zechariah warned the people who had just begun rebuilding the temple that they were to listen to God's message through the prophets. They were also to keep a close relationship with God so there would be no future judgment.

This opening message is followed by visions that offered encouragement to the builders at a time when they were ready to give up. Zechariah comforted them by telling them God had a long-term plan for Israel.

In chapters 7and 8, Zechariah calls the people to obey God by acting fairly and mercifully to one another. God wanted obedience in his relationship with them.

Chapters 9–14 tell of the coming Messiah, the last judgment, and the long-term growth of the final kingdom.

Outline of Contents:

The Call to Obedience (1:1–1:6)
Visions (1:7–6:15)
Obedience Versus Legalism (7:1–8:23)
Judgment on Israel's Enemies (9:1–8)
The Coming of Zion's King (Jesus) (9:9–14:21)

MALACHI

Introduction:

This book records the messages of the prophet, Malachi, who lived during the second half of the fifth century BC, after the temple had been rebuilt. The Jews' religious life was not in good condition. They had married foreign women, failed to give God what they should have, and even left God.

Malachi's chief concern was that the Israelites' relationship to God was not as it should be. They had forgotten God and treated Him with dishonor. They failed to do what God required of them. Because of this, there would be judgment, but the God-fearing people did not need to worry because they were in God's book and would enjoy God's salvation forever.

Outline of Contents:

God's Love for Israel (1:1–5)
Israel Insults God (1:6–2:16)
God's Judgment and Promise (2:17–4:6)

NEW TESTAMENT

In the New Testament, God fulfills the promises He made to His people in the Old Testament.

This cross lights up our yard during Easter Week.
From the author's personal collection.

Matthew

Introduction:

The book of Matthew tells of the good news that the long-awaited Messiah had come to save the people—both Jews and Gentiles. Matthew, one of the twelve disciples, is believed to be the author of this book. It was probably written sometime before the Romans destroyed the temple in Jerusalem in 70 AD,

Although Mark and Luke also wrote about Jesus' life, Matthew's Gospel has some special things that are different from the others. Matthew uses much of the Gospel to show that Jesus is the promised Messiah of the Old Testament. Matthew quotes the Old Testament often and uses the phrase "kingdom of heaven" from the Old Testament frequently. Because of this, many people think he was writing his Gospel to Jewish people. Matthew also presents Christ as the great teacher who helps us understand God's law and tells the people about the kingdom of God and what it is. Most of Christ's teachings are found in the following five places.

1. The Sermon on the Mount (5:1-7:27)
2. Instruction to the Disciples (10:5-42)
3. Teaching through Parables (13:3-52)
4. The Meaning of Discipleship (18:1-35)
5. Teachings about the End of Time and the
   Coming of the Kingdom of Heaven (24:4–25:46)

Outline of Contents:

Background and Preparation (1:1–4:25)
The Galilean Ministry (5:1–18:35)
The Sermon on the Mount (5:1–7:29)
The Ministry through Miracles (8:1–10:42)
Teaching through Parables (11:1–13:52)
Opposition and Withdrawal (13:53–16:12)
Jesus as the Son of God (16:13–18:35)
The Final Period (19:1–28:20)
Toward Jerusalem (19:1–20:34)
The Triumphal Entry (21:1–17)
Christ as Teacher (21:18–25:46)
Trial, Death, and Burial (26:1–27:66)
Resurrection and Ascension (28:1–20)

MARK

Mark, the author of this Gospel, probably was the first to write down the events of Jesus' life. It is believed that he is the same person who worked for many years as a missionary with Paul and Barnabas. The book of Mark, which stresses facts and actions rather than themes of topics, is the most exciting account of the life of Christ among the Gospels. Although it is the shortest of the four Gospels, it is often the most detailed. From the beginning, Mark tells the stories of Christ's ministry, especially his miracles.

Mark shows Jesus as a man of action and authority. He spends one third of the book telling the events of Christ's last week on earth, ending with the Savior's death and resurrection.

Outline of Contents:

Background and Preparation (1:1–13)
Ministry of Healing and Teaching (1:14–8:26)
Jesus and his Disciples (8:27–10:45)
Jericho and Jerusalem (10:46–13:37)
Passion and Death of Christ (14:1–15:47)
The Resurrected Christ and His Followers (16:1–20)

LUKE

Introduction:

Luke, the longest of the Gospels, was written by the same author as the book of Acts. Luke's writing shows him to be a highly-educated man who wrote from a Greek background and viewpoint.

Luke tells us in the first four verses of his book that he wrote this Gospel so we would have the true and complete story of Jesus' life. He wrote the fullest, most orderly story of Jesus' life.

One of Luke's interests in writing this book was to show that Jesus loved all kinds of people. He often wrote about and identified by name the women Christ met and spoke to. He also gave more attention to children than any other gospel writer. In the parables, especially, he wrote about the poor and oppressed. Jesus is shown by Luke as an actual person in history who "came to seek and to save what was lost" (19:10).

The theme of joy is felt throughout this book, from the song of Mary and the angels at Jesus' birth to the disciples who "returned to Jerusalem with great joy" after Christ's ascension. It is obvious that Luke wanted to tell the good news of Christ and show that his coming brought joy as well as hope and salvation to a sinful world.

Outline of Contents:

Introduction (1–1:4)
Birth and Childhood of John the Baptist and of Jesus (1:5–2:52)
Ministry of John the Baptist (3:1–20)
Jesus' Baptism and Temptation (3:21–4:12)
Jesus' Teaching and Healing Ministry (4:13–9:50)
Jesus' Mission (9:51–18:30)
Suffering and Crucifixion of Jesus (18:31–23:56)
Resurrection and Ascension (24:1–53)

John

Introduction:

The fourth Gospel was also written by one of Jesus' twelve disciples, John, the disciple whom Jesus loved. John wrote this Gospel sometime between 90–100 AD so that "you may believe that Jesus is the Christ, the Son of God, and that by believing you may have life in his name" (John 20:31).

Although the book of John gives a general outline of the life and work of Jesus Christ, it is very different from the other three Gospels. John reports five miracles that are not reported by the other Gospels. Only two of the miracles reported in the other Gospels are reported in John. This book contains no parables and seems to stress Jesus' relationships with individuals.

The purpose of this Gospel is to report the signs, usually called miracles in other Gospels. The signs that John reports give proof that Christ is God and has supernatural powers. Although John gives much attention to providing that Jesus is the Son of God, he also shows often that Jesus was very much a human by showing that he was tired, sad, hungry, and loving.

Outline of Contents:

Prologue and Theme (1:1–18)
Introduction of Jesus (1:19–4:54)
Jesus' Ministry as God's Son (5:1–10:42)
Crises in Jerusalem (11:1–12:50)
Jesus with His Disciples (13:1–17:26)
Trial, Death, and Burial (18:1–19:42)
Resurrection and Conclusion (20:1–21:25)

THE ACTS OF THE APOSTLES

Introduction:

The Acts of the Apostles is the second part of Luke's history. It was written so we would have the true story of how the Christian church began and grew.

This book tells about the work of two of the apostles—Peter and Paul. Peter is the central person involved in beginning the Church in Jerusalem, and Paul is the important missionary who went out to nearby countries to tell others about Christ. Acts can also be called "The Acts of the Holy Spirit" because it teaches about the coming and work of the Spirit.

The book of Acts teaches three things about the early church:

1) What the message of the early Church was
2) How the Jews rejected this message and how God sent the apostles to the Gentiles, who accepted it
3) How the early church was treated by the local and Roman governments

Outline of Contents:

Paul's Mission in Rome (27:1–28:31)

Suzanne's note: This book is very easy to read and is very important to Christians because it tells us who believe that Christ is our Savior that we should be spreading the Gospel "to the ends of the earth." Jesus' last words on earth, just before He was taken up into heaven, were "You will receive power when the Holy Spirit comes on you; and you will be my witnesses in Jerusalem, and in all Judea and Samaria and to the ends of the earth" (Acts 1:8).

Romans

Introduction:

This letter was written by Paul to the church in Rome in 56 or 57 AD as he was finishing his third missionary journey. Paul had hoped to first go to Jerusalem and then on to Rome and Spain. He probably writes this letter in preparation for his visit.

The theme of this letter is righteousness. Paul teaches in this letter that (1) no human being is righteous, (2) Jesus Christ is perfectly righteous, (3) if we have faith in Jesus, we are freed from the power of sin, given a new life, and returned to a right relationship with God, and (4) we should live Christian lives that are "holy and pleasing to God."

Outline of Contents:

Introduction (1–1:17)
No One is Righteous (1:18–3:20)
Righteousness is Through Faith (3:21–8:39)
Israel in God's Plan (9:1–11:36)
Christian Living and Relationships (12:1–15:13)
Conclusion and Greetings (15:14–16:27)

1 Corinthians

Suzanne's note: Paul is very repetitious; but it is important to know that he is on fire for the Lord Jesus Christ. The people (especially in the Church of Corinth) are so obstinate that Paul feels it is his duty to make things very clear, thus he repeats and repeats himself. He is boldly standing up for Christ. This will ultimately leave an impression on the reader. I doubt that there will be much boredom in Paul's upcoming letters. Let's keep in mind what Paul goes through as he travels from church to church, writing letters in advance to warn the people that he will be with them soon and that he is hopeful that they will change their wicked ways.

Introduction:

This letter is sixteen chapters long and was written by Paul to the church in Corinth, probably in the winter of 55 AD. It was while he was in Ephesus that he sent this letter in response to a letter from the Corinthian church.

Located on the Mediterranean, the city of Corinth was a wealthy trading center. It was also a wicked city and was known for that throughout the Roman world. Because the church in Corinth was new, it was hard for the Christians there not to act like their neighbors, so the church had some problems.

The Christians in Corinth were not getting along with one another. They were taking sides. Some of them were living very sinful lives. Paul wrote this letter to scold them and teach them how Christians should act. He tried to teach practical lessons about the Christian life so that people in Corinth would know right from wrong.

Outline of Contents:

2 Corinthians

Introduction:

This letter, known as 2 Corinthians, seems to have been written a few months after the first letter. The divisions and problems that were present in 1 Corinthians were still in the church at Corinth. Paul, himself, may have made a quick trip to Corinth, but he left rather quickly because some of the members in the church there refused to change or believe that Paul truly was an apostle of God.

After returning to Macedonia, Paul felt much better when Titus brought him the good news that the people in the Corinthian church had seen their problems and sins and were willing to change. It was at this time that Paul wrote his second letter to the Corinthians.

The first part of this letter tells how happy and thankful Paul was when he heard that the Corinthians were sorry for the way they had acted and were now trying to live the way God wanted them to.

In the second part of the letter, Paul defends himself against the people who were angry with him and who were saying untrue things about him.

Outline of Contents:

Introduction (1:1–11)
Paul as God's Messenger (1:12–7:16)
Generosity in Giving (8:1–9:15)
Paul as an Apostle (10:1–13:10)
Conclusion (13:11–14)

Galatians

Introduction:

Paul wrote this letter to the Christian churches in the Roman province of Galatia. These churches being confused by false teachers, called Judaizers, who were teaching the gentile Christians that they were not really saved unless they obeyed all the Jewish laws such as circumcision, eating special foods, and celebrating Jewish feast days. This group also said that Paul did not have God's authority, and, therefore, was not to be listened to. Paul begins the letter by telling the Galatians what gospel it is that he teaches and that his authority is from God. We cannot be saved from our sins by obeying the law; we are saved only by believing in Jesus Christ. Christians are free to live by the law of love, not the Law of Moses. Paul says that faith must be shown in love, and believers must live by the Spirit.

Outline of Contents:

Introduction (1:1–10)
Paul's Authority from God (1:11–2:21)
Legalism versus God's Grace (3:1–4:31)
The Gospel in Practice—(5:1–6:16)
Conclusion (6:17–18)

Ephesians

Suzanne's note: In the New Testament, in Paul's letter to the Ephesians 4:26b-27, Paul says " ... Do not let the sun go down while you are still angry and do not give the devil a foothold."

This photo is a sunset from the author's home.

Introduction:

This letter was written by Paul during his two-year imprisonment in Rome in about 60 AD. This letter probably was sent not just to the church at Ephesus but also to all the Christian churches near Ephesus. Ephesus was a large, important city at that time, so it was a natural center for the Christian churches.

One of Paul's themes in Ephesians is that of unity and God's purpose to bring all things in heaven and on earth together under one head, even Christ. Because of this unity, all Christians are one family in Jesus, and they should act with love toward each other. He gives believers instructions on how to live a life of love by addressing the husband/wife, parent/child, and master/slave relationships.

In this letter, Paul also writes about the Church—not a church building in a certain place, but a church that is made up by all Christians who have ever lived. We call this "the Church universal." He compares Christ's relationship to the Church to the body, to a building, and to a wife.

Outline of Contents:

Greetings (1:1–2)
Christ and the Church (1:3–3:21)
Conduct of the Believer (4:1–6:9)
The Christian's Warfare (6:10–20)
Conclusion (6:21–24)
Suzanne's note: May you all grow in a deeper love for Christ and each other through Paul's messages.

Philippians

Introduction:

Philippians, as well as Colossians, Philemon, and Ephesians, was written by Paul while he was in prison in Rome in about 60 AD. The Philippians had sent Epaphroditus to Paul with a gift. While Epaphroditus was in Rome, he became sick, and the Philippian Christians were worried about him. After Epaphroditus recovered, Paul sent him back to Philippi with this letter.

Paul's strong feelings of love for the Philippians is felt throughout this letter, and this is the most personal of Paul's letters written to a church. Paul tells of his thankfulness for the love and helpfulness of the Philippians.

Even though Paul was writing this letter from prison, this letter is full of joy. The words "joy" and "rejoice" are used fourteen times. Paul gives his own testimony to the meaning of his present life when he writes, "For to me, to live is Christ, and to die is gain" (1:21).

As in his other letters, Paul gives words of encouragement and instructions for living in harmony with others and in obedience to God.

Outline of Contents:

Introduction (1:1–11)
Paul's Circumstances and Concern (1:12–30)
Imitating Christ's Humility (2:1–18)
Paul's Messengers (2:19–30)
Warnings and Advice (3:1–4:20)
Conclusion (4:21–23)

COLOSSIANS

Introduction:

Colossians is Paul's third letter written from prison in Rome. Epaphras had come to Rome and told Paul that there were false teachers in Colosse who were telling the people that the Christian faith was incomplete. They were teaching the Colossians to worship angels and to follow special rules and ceremonies.

Paul wrote to the Colossians to oppose these false teachers. He reminded them that Jesus is supreme over everything, that his death is all we need to save us from our sins, and that through him we are free from man-made rules.

Outline of Contents:

Greetings and Appreciation (1:1–8)
Christ and the Believer (1:9–2:5)
Dangerous Rules (2:6–23)
Rules for Holy Living (3:1–4:6)
Greetings and Conclusion (4:7–18)

1 Thessalonians

Introduction:

Paul started the Church at Thessalonica on his second missionary journey. He taught there for about three weeks, but then had to leave because the Jews were opposing him so strongly. On hearing from Timothy about the conditions in Thessalonica, Paul wrote this letter from Corinth in 51 AD to encourage the Thessalonians and to teach them more about Christianity.

Paul begins by praising the Thessalonians for being brave and not giving up their faith "in spite of severe suffering". He instructs them "how to live in order to please God" 2:4. In addition, he teaches them about Jesus' second coming. He explains that the time of Jesus' coming is secret, so they should keep working hard until he comes.

Outline of Contents:

Introduction and Thanksgiving (1:1–10)
Paul's Ministry in the Church (2:1–3:13)
Instructions on the Lord's Coming (4:1–5:11)
Conclusion (5:12–28)

2 Thessalonians

Suzanne's note: Keep in mind that these letters were written just fifty-one years after Christ left the earth. Christianity was very new to the people, and most of the Jews did not believe in Jesus as the Savior of the world. Paul was trying very hard to pass on his beliefs through friends of his who became believers and by his own journeys to the different churches in that area.

Introduction:

2 Thessalonians was sent from Corinth a few months after the first letter. Some people had misunderstood Paul and were sure Jesus was coming very soon. In fact, they had stopped working and were just waiting for Jesus.

Paul writes the Thessalonians again and describes to them what Jesus' second coming will be like. He also reminds them to keep working hard until Jesus comes and to use their time wisely.

Outline of Contents:

Paul's Personal Concern (1:1–12)
Conditions for the Lord's Coming (2:1–17)
Strong Advice and a Blessing (3:1–18)

1 Timothy

Suzanne's note: Check out the scripture passage in 2 Timothy 3:16. "All Scripture is God-breathed and is useful for teaching, rebuking, correcting and training in righteousness, so that the man of God may be thoroughly equipped for every good work."

Introduction:

1 and 2 Timothy and Titus are commonly called Pastoral Letters because they deal with the qualifications and duties of pastors.

Timothy was born in Lystra and had a Greek father and a Jewish mother who taught him Scriptures from childhood. He went with Paul on his second missionary journey, and from then on helped in his work. At the time Paul wrote this letter, Timothy was working as the teacher and leader of the church at Ephesus.

Timothy was quite young to have the important job of leading a church, so Paul wrote this very personal letter to him. In this letter, Paul gives him help and advice for his work. He warns him of false teachers and their teachings that are opposite God's commands. Because of Paul's deep care for Timothy, he offers him advice on how to be a man of God.

Outline of Contents:

Introduction (1:1–17)
Instructions for the Church (1:18–3:16)
Personal Instructions for Timothy (4:1–6:21)

2 Timothy

Paul was probably arrested again sometime after writing 1 Timothy and Titus, and he likely wrote this second letter to Timothy from Rome where he was being held a prisoner. In this letter, Paul seems to know that there is little chance of his getting out of prison and that he will soon die. It is for these reasons that he writes to Timothy.

Paul wants not only to see Timothy again, but also to encourage him because he would have to continue Paul's missionary work after Paul's death.

Paul gives Timothy more instructions on how to lead a church and warns him to stay away from false teachers. He urges Timothy to be faithful to true Christian teachings.

Outline of Contents:

Greeting (1:1–2)
Encouragement to be Faithful (1:3–2:13)
The False and the True Way (2:14–3:9)
Paul's Charge to Timothy (3:10–4:8)
Conclusion (4:9–22)

Titus

Introduction:

Titus was another friend and helper of Paul's. He traveled with Paul on some of his missionary journeys and was working as a leader of the church at Crete. This letter is similar to the two letters to Timothy.

The church in Crete seems to have been an unorganized church and made up of people who need much instruction in being Christians. Paul tells Titus and the church how God's people should behave. He tells Titus to teach the people the truth of God and instructs him in how to be a good leader of the Church.

Outline of Contents:

Introduction (1:1–4)
Duties of Elders and Deacons (1:5–16)
Duties of a Pastor (2:1–3:11)
Conclusion (3:12–15)

Philemon

Introduction:

Philemon was a leader of the church at Colosse and a friend of Paul's. Philemon's slave, Onesimus, had stolen money from him and had run away to Rome. While he was there, he met Paul and became a Christian.

Paul sends Onesimus back to Philemon with this letter. He begs Philemon to forgive Onesimus and to treat him as a brother in Christ instead of a runaway slave.

This short letter combines with Ephesians, Colossians, and Philippians to form the "prison letters" because they were written while Paul was in prison in Rome for the first time.

Outline of Contents:

Greetings (1–3)
Paul's Concern and Love (4–7)
Paul's Plea for Onesimus (8–22)
Farewell (23–25)

Hebrews

Introduction:

Although the author of Hebrews is unknown, it was probably written in the late seventh decade AD. During this time, persecution was a real problem for the church in Rome. This letter was most likely written to the Jewish Christians in either Palestine or Rome who were ready to give up their faith and return to the Jewish faith because of persecution. Hebrews was written to teach these Jewish Christians that the Christian faith is better in every way than the Jewish faith. Christ is from God and is better than the angels, Moses and Joshua, and any priest, and he is the only complete sacrifice. The author shows how Jesus completed the Jewish faith by making the final sacrifice for sin. After his death, none of the Old Testament sacrifices were needed.

Chapter 11, the famous chapter on men and women of faith in the Old Testament times, must have given these persecuted Christians great hope and helped them to have faith and trust in God.

Outline of Contents:

Christ: God's Complete Revelation (1:1–3)
Christ: Superior to Angels (1:4–2:18)
Christ: Superior to Moses and Joshua (3:1–4:13)
Christ: The Superior Intercessor or Priest
(4:14–7:28)
Christ's Superior Covenant and Sacrifice
(8:1–10:18)
The Practical Appeal (10:19–12:29)
Concluding Advice—(13:1–25)

James

Introduction:

The book of James may be the earliest of the New Testament letters, written in about 48 AD. This letter, written by Jesus' brother, one of the leaders of the church in Jerusalem, was addressed to Christians everywhere. The seven books of the new testament from James through Jude are called the general letters because they were written to Christians in general and not to a specific church.

James wrote this letter to teach Christians the practice of Christianity. He insists that if we have real faith, we will show it by acting like Christians. He gives practical advice on things like anger and quarreling, showing favoritism, controlling the tongue, boasting, patience, and prayer.

Outline of Contents:

The Heart of True Religion (1:1–27)
True Faith in Practice (2:1–3:12)
True Wisdom in Practice (3:13–5:12)
The Prayer of Faith (5:13–20)

1 Peter

Introduction:

1 Peter was written by Peter, one of Jesus' twelve disciples, to the Christians who lived in the northern part of Asia Minor. These Christians were being persecuted for their faith, so Peter wrote to encourage them.

He urges them to remember how much Jesus suffered for them and to follow His example by trusting God to care for them. Because God chose them to be His people and because Jesus suffered and died for them, Peter then tells these Christians they should live holy lives. He goes on to tell them how they can live as Christians in this sinful world and have hope for the future.

Outline of Contents:

Greetings (1:1–2)
Praise to God for Salvation (1:3–12)
Holy Living (1:13–2:12)
Conduct of the Believer (2:13–4:11)
Ministry through Suffering (4:12–5:11)
Conclusion (5:12–14)

2 Peter

Introduction:

2 Peter was written in about 66 AD to the same group of Christians as Peter's first letter. These Christians were no longer in danger of persecution, but they were in danger of being confused by false teachers.

Peter reminds the Christians that the best way to resist false teachers is to grow in the knowledge and practice of the Christian faith. He warns them that God will destroy the false teachers. Because Jesus will certainly keep His promise to come again, Peter reminds these Christians to live "holy and godly lives." 3:11

Outline of Contents:

Introduction (1:1–2)
True Knowledge (1:3–21)
False Teachers and Their Destruction (2:1–22)
The Day of the Lord (3:1–18)

1 John

Introduction:

1, 2, and 3 John were written by John, the beloved disciple, who also wrote the fourth Gospel. All four books may have been written about the same time, probably about 90 AD.

The first letter of John was written to warn Christians about dangerous false teachers who were trying to mislead them. These teachers were teaching that the man Jesus was not the Christ, the Son of God. They said that God did not become man. John tells the Christians he is writing because it is very important to know and believe that Jesus Christ is both God and man. John also encourages these Christians to keep their faith in Christ strong and to continue loving one another. He says Christians can know they are God's children if they love one another and obey God's commands.

Outline of Contents:

Introduction (1:1–4)
Walking in the Light (1:5–2:29)
Love Must Fill our Lives (3:1–4:21)
Faith and Freedom from Doubts (5:1–12)
Conclusion (5:13–21)

2 John

Introduction:

In this letter, John writes how important it is for Christians to love one another. He says that to love means to obey God's commandments, and God's commandments tell us to live lives of love.

John again emphasizes the importance of the doctrine that Jesus is God's Son and both man and God. Christians should separate themselves from those who teach that Jesus is not God's Son.

Outline of Contents:

Greeting (1–3)
Advice and Warning (4–11)
Conclusion (12–13)

3 John

Introduction:

John wrote 3 John to Gaius, his friend and a leader in the church. There was a man named Diotrephes in Gaius's church who was refusing to welcome God's messengers. John writes this letter to praise and thank Gaius for his help and to scold Diotrephes for not cooperating. John promises to come to this church soon to deal with this matter himself.

Outline of Contents:

JUDE

Introduction:

Jude, like James, was a brother of Jesus. He wrote to warn Christians about the same false teachers Peter wrote about in his second letter. These false teachers were not only teaching that Jesus was not the Son of God; they were also leading the people to live sinful lives. Jude warns that God will punish and destroy these false teachers just as he had punished sinners in the Old Testament.

Outline of Contents:

Introduction (1–2)
Warnings against False Teachers (3–16)
Warning and Conclusion (17–25)

Revelation

Introduction:

The book of Revelation was written by the apostle John during his exile on the island of Patmos. John's purpose in writing this book was to give hope and encouragement to those Christians who were suffering severe persecution for their faith in Jesus Christ. These Christians needed to know that God controls whatever happens here on earth.

Through the imagery and symbols, even though they are sometimes difficult to understand, one thing is made clear: Jesus Christ is the Lord and ruler over everyone and everything, even powerful human governments. He is clearly in control and will someday judge and punish what is evil, even Satan. He will also establish an everlasting kingdom with a new heaven and a new earth.

Outline of Contents:

Christ Reveals Himself to John (1:1–20)
Letters to the Seven Churches (2:1–3:22)
The Heavenly Throne (4:1–5:14)
The Seven Seals (6:1–8:5)
The Seven Trumpets (8:6–11:19)
The Seven Figures (12:1–14:20)
The Bowls of Wrath (15:1–16:21)
Babylon Judged (17:1–19:10)
Beast and False Prophet Judged (19:11–21)
Satan Judged (20:1–3)
Thousand-Year Reign (20:4–6)
Rebellion and Final Judgment(20:7–15)

New Heaven, New Earth, New Jerusalem
(21:1–22:5)

Conclusion (22:6–21)

Suzanne's note: The entire book of Revelations is a *revelation of Jesus Christ to His people.* Though it is a difficult book to understand, remember, we will not understand everything here on earth. *Do not be afraid of this book.* Read it and consume what God reveals to you. If you do not understand and really want to, seek out someone who has thoroughly studied this book.

May you all enjoy God's peace and love in your lives.

Bonus

Favorite Family Recipes

Mom's Banana Bread

1 cup sugar
1 stick of oleo (Butter)
2 eggs
3 ripe bananas (mashed)
8 Tbsp. sour milk (½ tsp. vinegar will make milk sour)
1 tsp. baking soda
2½ cups flour
⅛ tsp. salt
½ cup chopped pecans or walnuts (optional)

1. Add baking soda to sour milk, and add salt to flour.
2. Add milk and flour alternately to sugar.
3. Combine sugar, oleo, eggs, and bananas. Beat well.
4. Bake at 350 degrees for 1 hour.

Dad's Old Fashioned Vegetable Soup

Soup bone with soup meat
3 carrots
3 stalks of celery
2 medium onions
Small amount of shredded cabbage
2 medium peeled potatoes, diced
1 bay leaf (remove after 15–20 min.)
1 small can of tomatoes
1 Tbsp. parsley
1 tsp. basil leaves
Garlic salt, salt, and pepper to taste

1. Wash meat and bone in cold water. Cover in cold water and bring to hard boil. Lower heat and skim scum several times until gone.
2. Add one whole onion and simmer. Remove meat from stock. Strain stock through cheesecloth and place stock in refrigerator overnight.
3. Remove meat from bone and carefully trim off the fat. Put meat in plastic bag in refrigerator.
4. Next day: Remove all fat from broth. Add meat.
5. Add diced vegetables and seasoning. Simmer for one hour (until veggies are tender).
6. Serve with noodles or dumplings.

Bill Sund's Savory Pot Roast

2 lbs. marbled chuck roast, seasoned to taste
6 celery stalks
1½ tbsp. Worcestershire sauce
Celery leaves
Sweet onions (cut into chunks)
Baking potatoes (peeled, cut into chunks)
Carrots (cut into chunks)
Celery (cut into chunks)
A-1 Steak Sauce
1 cup red cooking wine

1. Spray covered roasting pan with cooking spray.
2. Place six celery stalks in bottom of pan.
3. Place raw roast on top of celery.
4. Sprinkle with 1½ Tbsp. Worcestershire Sauce
5. Cover top of roast with celery leaves.
6. Add chunks of sweet onions, peeled baker potatoes, carrots, more celery; arrange vegetables around roast.
7. Pour small amount A-1 Sauce over meat only.
8. Pour 1 cup red cooking wine over everything.
9. Bake in middle of oven at 325 degrees for two hours, uncovered for last thirty minutes.

Suzy's Salsa

3 tomatoes, chopped
1 small sweet onion, chopped
2 celery stalks, chopped
1 Tbsp. minced garlic
¾ tsp. salt
Dash of pepper
Cilantro leaves to taste
⅛ cup fresh squeezed limejuice (bottled juice okay)
Optional: ¼ cup Heinz Chili Sauce, black beans, and/or pineapple chunks

1. Combine all ingredients and serve with Lime Chips.

PATTI'S BEST CHERRY CHEESE CAKE

2–8 oz. packages of cream cheese, softened
1 cup powdered sugar
8 oz. Cool Whip
1 graham cracker crust
1 can cherry pie filling

1. Beat cream cheese and sugar until smooth.
2. Fold in the Cool Whip and spoon onto the crust.
3. Top with pie filling and refrigerate.

Jeanne's Crock Pot Chicken

4 chicken breasts
1 large Onion, sliced in thick rings
Baby carrots
10 oz. can cream of chicken soup
10 oz. can cheesy broccoli soup
1 can whole potatoes

1. Put carrots and potatoes in bottom of crock pot.
2. Put chicken breasts on top of vegetables.
3. Put onion rings on top of chicken.
4. Mix two cans of soup together and pour over all.
5. Bake on low for 6 hours.

Kathryn's Cauliflower
Mashed Potatoes

Potatoes
1 head of cauliflower
Butter, cream cheese, cheddar cheese, salt, pepper, and parsley

1. Optional: garlic or other herbs. Steam a head of cauliflower and mash with cooked potatoes to desired consistency.
2. Add butter, cream cheese, salt, and fresh-ground black pepper to taste.
3. Grate cheese and fresh parsley over the top of the potatoes.
    Optional: add garlic or other herbs.